Animal Miracles

Inspirational and Heroic
True Stories

Brad Steiger
&
Sherry Hansen Steiger

ADAMS MEDIA CORPORATION
Holbrook, Massachusetts

Published by
Adams Media Corporation
260 Center Street, Holbrook, MA 02343

ISBN: 1-58062-122-8

Printed in the United States of America.

First Edition
J I H G F E D C B A

Library of Congress Cataloging-in-Publication Data
Steiger, Brad.
Animal miracles : inspirational and heroic true stories /
Brad Steiger and Sherry Hansen Steiger. —1st edition.
p. cm.
ISBN 1-58062-122-8
1. Animal heroes—Anecdotes. 2. Pets—Anecdotes.
I. Steiger, Sherry Hansen. II. Title.
SF416.S75   1999
636—dc21   98-48355
CIP

Illustration by Jean Cassels/Publishers Graphics.

*This book is available at quantity discounts for bulk purchases.
For information, call 1-800-872-5627
(in Massachusetts, 781-767-8100).*

Visit our home page at http://www.adamsmedia.com

Preface

Deep within the soul of Man, there resides a secret longing for a savior of mythic proportions.

Both the enduring popularity of the Greek classics, which feature larger-than-life protagonists, and the contemporary obsession with "superheroes" such as Superman, Batman, Spiderman, testify to this ongoing yearning that is, in itself, a hallmark of our collective psyche.

The characteristics of these idols consistently fulfill the same criteria: defenders of righteousness; champions of the meek and defenseless; undaunted courage; unflagging physical stamina; infinite patience; unequivocal loyalty. And, miraculously, an uncanny penchant for always appearing at the right place . . . just in the nick of time!

Philosophers or theologians might posit that the reason why the contemporary imagination is captured by this particular expression of longing, is because it represents our own individual quest for God, sublimated into human form. Or, psychologists might very well theorize that we are searching for the lost communion we had with Mother or Father during our infancy; the delicious sense that they were the Source of All—salvation included.

Whatever the explanation, the fact remains that many of us do indeed harbor a "rescue fantasy," which we project onto other people. Only recently has this concept expanded to include under its rubric our furry, feathered friends, who have undergone a profound transformation in our public consciousness.

Indeed, it is only in the last several years that contemporary society has restored to animals the powers, virtues, abilities, and attributes that had been originally assigned to them in ancient times but disappeared over the centuries. (Remember Remus and Romulus being suckled by the wolf? The Dove sent by Noah as messenger?) We have reawakened ourselves to the vital and different roles that animals can play in our lives—sometimes with significant, even life-changing consequences. Veils of mystery and misunderstanding are being lifted rapidly, as we regain a newfound appreciation of the divine spark that flows throughout the universe, including "all creatures large and small."

Scientific research, sometimes dry and unappealing, has been bolstered by personal anecdotes lavish with beauty and drama, many of which you'll find in this inspiring book. After reading the genuinely amazing stories contained within, you will assuredly come away with a different regard for animals, something bordering close to reverence, perhaps. Your perspective will be undeniably changed.

As a child with allergies, including a severe reaction to animal hair, I was unfortunately precluded from the joyous position of being a pet owner. In fact, I almost had an outright aversion to animals, based on the knowledge that their proximity guaranteed an immediate eruption of hives and coughing fits. My acquaintance with the deep spiritual bond that exists between Man and Animal was, consequently, severely limited.

But when I began collecting stories for *Small Miracles* and *Small Miracles II*, I discovered first-hand just how deep that connection is. I encountered a story told by eminent psychiatrist Carl Jung, in which flocks of birds repeatedly gathered at the windows of dying souls, signifying their spiritual transition. Another story reported by Jung told of the sudden appearance of a rare "golden scarab" at his window, at precisely the moment his patient was recounting her own peculiar dream about . . . a golden scarab! and the psychological breakthrough this synchronicity precipitated.

After collecting these and other true stories, my own position was irrevocably altered. I learned to regard animals with a greater degree of respect than I had previously, and, to believe, with even more fervor than before, that in life, everything is possible.

The wondrous tales in this book center on miraculous rescue operations achieved by both docile pets and formidable beasts-of-the-wild. When you read the accounts of humans being released from the jaws of death and delivered up to salvation by animal heroes, you will be awestruck and humbled, filled with a sense of mystery that such accounts must ultimately evoke. You will undoubtedly begin to recognize and honor your own interconnectedness with our animal friends and the ties that bind us forever.

And the next time you're in a tight spot, before yelling "Superman!" you might very well call for Fido instead. Chances are a furry friend will be there first!

Yitta Halberstam
New York City
November 1998

Introduction

On July 28, 1998, a Newfoundland terrier named Maui became a French national hero when he gave his life to rescue three tourists from drowning in rough Mediterranean waters off the southern tip of Corsica. Maui managed to tow a lifeguard's surfboard towards shore with the exhausted swimmers—two Dutch and one British—clinging to it for their lives. Then, just as they reached the beach, crashing waves descended on them. Firemen who had been called to the beach managed to complete the rescue and bring the three tourists to safety, but Maui, physically spent from his Herculean efforts, drowned.

The great American philosopher Ralph Waldo Emerson once observed that "God has delegated Himself to a million deputies." The magnificent, self-sacrificing Newfoundland terrier Maui was surely one of God's deputy miracle workers.

One of the greatest miracles that animals give us is the gift of unconditional love. As many an animal lover has acknowledged, "I know my pet would give its life for me. Would I give my life for my pet?"

Why do our pets love us so? Are they simply more noble than we? Or, as the cynic might ask, are they just more simpleminded?

Well, perhaps their less complex thinking permits them to glimpse more clearly the great revelation of the

Oneness of all life. Perhaps their simple, loving hearts make it impossible for them to separate themselves from a kinship with the world around them.

In their book *The Strange World of Animals and Pets*, Vincent and Margaret Gaddis write that animals live in realms of their own—realms totally different and far older than ours. "They possess senses and extensions of senses that we have lost or never attained. They see sights that we shall never see. They hear sounds that we shall never hear. They respond to terrestrial and cosmic rhythms and cycles that we have never charted."

"Animals are intelligent beings with their own special awareness and wisdom," Penelope Smith asserts in her book *Animals . . . Our Return to Wholeness*. "There is a growing realization, an awakening cultural awareness, that we are all linked—physically, mentally, and spiritually."

On some level of consciousness, those of us who love animals have always sensed that there was a time when we humans experienced a much greater ability to communicate with the forces of nature around us. In that less sophisticated time, an era devoid of science and technology, people had to rely on their keen senses and intuitive powers in order to stay alive.

As humankind began more and more to abandon a natural existence, it exchanged a communion with nature and a sense of Oneness for partnerships with its own kind that would eventually bring about mutual protection and companionship. What a great tragedy it is that the great majority of us still consider it necessary to widen the chasm between the artificial reality of civilization and the natural world of kinship.

Kinship with all the creatures of the earth, sky, and water is an integral element in traditional Native American shamanic practices, and such a respect for all life forms is also manifest in the teachings of such Christian mystics as Saint Francis of Assisi and in the code of behavior embodied in traditional Jewish writings.

We (the authors) have long believed that angels may, when necessary, utilize a family pet to perform acts of bravery and heroism. On the other hand, we also know that ordinary tabbies and undistinguished mutts have suddenly risen to the occasion and accomplished miraculous deeds.

We are firm believers in miracles as well as in a spiritual connection between animals and humans, and sometimes we find ourselves becoming a bit impatient with those who don't seem to be able to appreciate the beautiful act of bonding with our animal companions.

Our friend Scott Smith, author of *Pet Souls*, believes that there are two kinds of people in the world—those who love animals and those who don't. "The latter cannot understand why the former lavish so much money and attention on their pets," Scott wrote in a letter to us. "That is simply because those who think of animals as 'things' have never bonded with an animal's personality or do not understand that it is no different from bonding with a human. Pets are like young children—their incapacities and vulnerabilities make them more, not less, endearing."

Because of our earlier books on the mysterious powers and abilities of animals (*Strange Powers of Pets*, *More Strange Powers of Pets*, *Cats Incredible*, and *The Mysteries of Animal Intelligence*), we have received hundreds of letters from our readers sharing their own inspirational accounts of human–animal interaction. And the number of personal accounts of miraculous experiences with animals increases wonderfully after each of our radio, television, or lecture appearances. And then there is the *Steiger Questionnaire of Mystical and Paranormal Experiences*, which we created in 1967 to provide us with our own sampling of contemporary expressions of the individual mystical experience. The questionnaire has now been distributed to over 30,000 correspondents, who have returned their reports to us with remarkable accounts of human lives forever changed because of miracles accomplished by animals. We will share a number of the most inspirational stories from our questionnaire in this book.

The stories that we have gathered for this collection tell of ordinary animals that accomplished extraordinary rescues, remarkable acts of heroism, and unselfish deeds of intervention. Such dramatic accounts give us hope that it is not too late—at least on the levels of mind and spirit—to reestablish the ancient realms of kinship with all life that we once maintained in our primeval innocence.

Sherry Hansen Steiger and Brad Steiger
Forest City, Iowa
September 1998

*W*hen we first bought our brightly colored macaw direct from the steaming jungles of South America in late September of 1982, my wife Cindy and I named him Cesar, after Cesar Romero, the handsome Latin American movie actor famous for his smooth, suave speaking voice.

But after we had had our parrot for a couple of weeks, we decided to rename him, because try as we might to get him to mimic any phrase at all—even a simple "hello"—we could only get him to whistle and, occasionally, to emit a loud, ear-piercing squawk. Cindy said it sounded to her like Stanley yelling for Stella in *A Streetcar Named Desire*, so she voted for Brando to replace Cesar as the bird's name.

One day when the parrot did "speak," he repeated the words over and over again in a low, jumbled mumble.

"What on earth was that supposed to be?" I asked when he first made those peculiar sounds.

Cindy laughed and said, "I think that was 'Hello, pretty, pretty bird.' At least that's what I've been repeating to him about five hundred times today."

The macaw's mumble capped it. We now had a parrot named Brando.

Even though we were disappointed with our inarticulate bird, the truth of the matter was that we had grown attached to Brando, whether he spoke clearly or not. He wasn't terribly messy, and he did have a winning twinkle in his eyes.

"He'll get better with time and as he grows more accustomed to our voices," Cindy, the eternal optimist, told me with great authority one evening when we were trying to coax a clearly articulated sound out of our mumbling parrot.

One night, about five or six weeks after we got Brando, I came home from work to find Cindy sitting in the easy chair next to his perch, a puzzled look on her face. "Since you beat me home from work, are you trying to decide what to fix for supper?" I teased her, knowing full well it was my night to cook.

Cindy put a finger to her lips, indicating a wish for silence, and nodded toward Brando.

I got very excited. Perhaps she had gotten him to speak something clearly and distinctly, something other than his usual unintelligible mumble.

As if on cue, the bird suddenly spoke out, clear as could be: "Help me! Please, someone help me!"

Now it was my turn to look puzzled. "Help me? What's that about?"

Cindy shrugged. "Our baby's first words. Aren't you proud?"

I slipped out of my coat and set my briefcase down next to my desk. "His first words and he wants someone to rescue him from us? That's gratitude for you. What were you doing to him before I got home? Plucking his tail feathers with your tweezers?"

Cindy rolled her large brown eyes and sighed in mock impatience at my lack of sensitivity. "We've got a mystery here, you big lug. Why would Brando's first clearly spoken words be a cry for help?"

I ran through the obvious answers. Had either of us left the television or radio on before leaving for work? Did Brando have some unresolved emotional or psychological issues of which we were unaware? Had Cindy herself screamed for help as she contemplated her mother's fast-approaching weekend visit for Thanksgiving?

"No, no, and no!" Cindy replied to my teasing questions. "But be quiet and listen a moment. I think I heard something else. I think I heard a voice coming from somewhere outside the house."

I sat down in the easy chair beside her and did as I was asked.

And then, after a few moments of silence, I heard it. A faint, faraway voice crying for help.

Once again, Brando was right on cue, providing us with an immediate echo: "Help me! Please, won't someone help me!"

I got out of the chair and headed for a window. After a momentary struggle with a stubborn latch, I had it open and was listening intently into the sounds of traffic on a chilly November evening.

"Please help me!"

There it was. Someone was clearly calling out for assistance.

"Help me!" Brando squawked at top lung and beak power. "Please help me!"

I told Cindy to call 911, and I went outside with a flashlight to investigate.

Rush hour was dying down, but there was still the din of traffic to contend with. Although the cries were easier to hear when I was outside, the hum of tires on pavement and the occasional blare of a horn made it difficult to determine exactly where the owner of the voice might be.

I investigated the line of bushes between our house and our neighbor's house, and I carefully directed the flashlight beam up and down our side of the street. After a few minutes, I was certain that I had pinpointed the cries as coming from a lot across the street where there now stood only a couple of old warehouses that would soon be torn down to make way for some new apartment complexes.

As I crossed the street, the person in distress obviously spotted my flashlight, for he called out, "Over here. I'm over here. Please help me!"

When I directed the beam toward the sound of the voice, I was shocked to see an older, white-haired gentleman pinned against the side of a building by a utility van.

Thankfully, at almost that same instant, the police car summoned by Cindy's 911 call arrived, and the officers, in turn, immediately called an ambulance.

The incredible story was that seventy-year-old Edward Kabrick, a semiretired plumber, had been using one of the old warehouses to store surplus equipment and supplies. He had gone out earlier that afternoon to pick up a used water softener for a customer's apartment. Somehow, as he walked toward the door of the warehouse, his old van slipped out of park and rolled down the incline, pinning him against the brick wall.

In terrible pain, Kabrick started yelling for help, but since he was only a couple of streets away from a busy road, no one heard him above the traffic noises. The poor man had suffered the agony of broken ribs and legs for hours, lapsing into unconsciousness, then waking again to cry out desperately for help. He had repeated the pitiful cycle for hours, growing weaker each time he regained consciousness.

Kabrick only worked part-time, so no one would particularly notice if he came into the office or not. His wife had passed away three years before, so there was no one at home to miss him if he didn't come home on schedule.

"I thought I would surely freeze to death if no one found me soon," he said, shaking my hand as they were placing him in the ambulance. "Thank you for hearing my cries for help. I didn't think that I would be able to last the night."

I told him that it was our parrot who deserved the thanks. Our mostly mute, mumbling parrot had apparently heard Kabrick earlier in the day when his voice was stronger, and then had clearly repeated the cries for help with the same urgency with which the trapped man had uttered them.

One of the police officers chuckled and shook his head in wonder. "You found Mr. Kabrick because your parrot repeated his cries for help? I would call that some kind of miracle."

I agreed. Why was it that good old Brando, a parrot that had never repeated a clearly distinct word until that day, had suddenly chosen to echo an injured man's desperate cries for help as loud and clear as could be?

"Yes," I told the officer. "I think that 'miracle' will be the next word we'll teach him."

Vance O.

In 1985, the summer of my eleventh year, the Kriemyers, who managed the supermarket on the edge of town, bought the old Victorian house across the street from us and announced their plans to tear it down and build their dream house on the lot.

Our normally quiet neighborhood was suddenly filled with excitement. Even before the wrecking crew arrived, a group of ladies from the local historical society picketed in front of the house, protesting its destruction. According to them, the stately old Victorian should be preserved and placed in a national directory of historic homes. Mr. and Mrs. Kriemyer were forced to make public statements on the radio and in the weekly newspaper informing people that experts from the university had declared the old Victorian simply a crumbling old house that had no real historical significance.

By mid-June, the house was rapidly disappearing before everyone's eyes. I braved saws and wrecking bars and angry men to snatch some historical treasures that had been abandoned in the musty attic—an old newspaper from 1900, a couple of magazines dated 1907, and eight colored glass bottles.

While I was rummaging in the uppermost reaches of the old place, the architecture bug really bit me hard. The workmen had already removed the roof, and as I was looking out over the neighborhood, I really began to admire the craftsmanship of the long-forgotten carpenters who had built the house in the 1890s.

So naturally, a month later, when the new crew of carpenters arrived to begin building the Kriemyers' dream house, I was right there to inspect every step of the construction process. I ignored the "Hey, kid, beat it" and "Bobby, go on home and bother your mommy" comments, for these men could not possibly understand that one day I would be a master architect. I might even hire them if they weren't too rude to me.

My beacon point of observation was once again the roof, and I got up there every chance I could. Which meant after the carpenters had quit for the day and there was no one around to chase me away.

Mr. Kriemyer caught me one night and complained to my dad, who gave me a severe warning to stay away from the construction site. Then, late one afternoon, one of the carpenters working overtime grabbed me by the ear and asked if I was trying to break my fool neck. He delivered me to my father, who threatened that I was not too big to get a spanking. Mom echoed the carpenter's rhetorical question about my trying to break my neck — or worse.

But there I was the next day, standing on a cross beam, trying to appear as confident and self-assured as the experienced carpenters did when they worked in that high place. All the workmen had gone home, and my only audience was Harley and Floyd, my two neighborhood buddies, and my mom, who was building up a fierce head of steam as she came running out of the house, screaming at me to get down at once.

I hadn't intended to oblige her quite so rapidly. But in a moment of total shock and terror I realized that I had lost my balance, and then I was plummeting toward the ground. From that height, I was certain to break any number of bones . . . and quite likely my neck.

But astonishingly, my fall was broken by a large white dog that literally came from nowhere and rushed beneath me to cushion my fall.

I was completely dazed by the impact with the big, furry body. Stars swirled around my eyes, and I couldn't breathe for a couple of minutes. Mom, Harley, and Floyd were hovering over me, each of them handling horror, relief, and gratitude in his or her own way as they saw that I appeared to be all right.

The big white dog stood there, panting, studying me curiously from a distance of three or four yards. It was as large as a German shepherd, a Great Dane, or some kind of cross between a Dalmatian and a shepherd. I couldn't identify the breed, but it was big. It had to have been a large dog to have broken my fall from that height without having injured itself. I suppose at that time I weighed about 105 pounds, so my body would have created quite an impact.

"Come here, boy," I called to him. "You saved my life!"

Very cautiously the dog drew nearer, as I talked it, step by step, into touching my outstretched hand. It gently licked my fingers, then turned and ran away.

We all called after it, promising it steaks and chops and any number of tasty rewards, but the big white dog never even turned around to acknowledge the offers we thought so tempting to any ordinary dog.

But that was the thing. We all agreed that this was no ordinary dog. It actually seemed as though it had accomplished its mission of saving me, and now it was on its way to perform another good deed or dramatic rescue.

Although I never did become an architect building houses, I became a social worker, hoping that I might help to reconstruct lives. I have always felt that the big white dog was my guardian angel in disguise—and that my life was saved so that I might try to accomplish something truly worthwhile with my own mission on Earth.

Robert S.

*J*oe is such an attentive canine caretaker that he saved Kim Lensing's life twice in less than a year.

Infant Kim was only ten days old when the young collie came running into the Lensings' bedroom and got Vicki Lensing to follow him back to the child's crib.

Vicki was horrified to find her baby blue in the face and lying very, very still. Thanks to Joe, she was in time to perform CPR on her infant daughter and save her life.

Ever since they had brought Kim home from the hospital, Vicki had felt uneasy about her baby's health, and she had asked their family doctor to examine the little girl very carefully. Although nothing was discovered that indicated any serious abnormality or medical condition in the infant, Vicki had noticed that even Joe seemed ill at ease and insisted on sleeping under Kim's crib.

Looking back on the frightening experience, Vicki told her husband Mark that it was as if Joe had known that their little daughter required special attention.

Such a demand for special attention arose again one night almost exactly eleven months later. Once again Joe came bounding into the master bedroom to awaken the sleeping mother.

"What's wrong with Joe?" Mark mumbled, barely managing to open both eyes. "Does he need to go outside?"

Vicki immediately picked up that Joe's sense of urgency had nothing to do with obeying the call of nature in the backyard. "I think he's worried about Kim," she explained to the back of her husband's head. Mark was already snoring again. He had been working an extra shift at the factory and she knew that he was dead tired.

Vicki got out of bed and followed Joe into Kim's bedroom. She gave her sleeping daughter a cursory once-over examination and decided that everything was fine.

But when she tried to return to bed, Joe blocked her path.

Vicki was puzzled and somewhat annoyed. How unlike the collie to be so aggressive and demanding. "Oh, all right," she sighed, yielding to Joe's obvious concern. "I'll check your little mistress again."

Under Joe's watchful eye, Vicki spent more time carefully examining her daughter. Nothing. Kim was fine. "She's okay, Joe," Vicki yawned. "I'm going back to bed."

But Joe, in collie body language, said no way.

"Come on, Joe," Vicki scowled, trying to push past him. "I'm tired. I don't take a dozen naps a day like a certain dog I know."

Joe kept at her until Vicki once again, this time quite irritated, went back to Kim's crib to conduct yet a third examination of her sleeping daughter.

It was during her third check of little Kim that Vicki discovered to her horror that her baby had stopped breathing—just like the time eleven months before. Once again she performed CPR—this time with Joe assisting her by licking Kim's face.

Later, Vicki and Mark learned, the doctors theorized that Joe's licking helped stimulate Kim to breathe again.

On this occasion, after the doctors completed their thorough examination of little Kim, their diagnosis revealed symptoms of a rare infant sleeping disorder.

Since the second frightening episode with its narrow escape, Kim sleeps with a special monitor that emits a beeping sound if she should stop breathing.

Joe is taking no chances, though. He still sleeps under Kim's bed.

*A*fter nearly thirty years my "shark toes" still occasionally shed the entire nail, and they remain more sensitive to pain than any of my other toes. But I don't complain. I was able to keep my foot, my leg, my entire body—thanks to the timely intervention of dolphins who protected me from a shark attack.

In 1968, while on ministerial internship at a Lutheran church in Austin, Texas, I was one of the few female staff members who assisted in planning and organizing a spiritual retreat for forty teenagers just off the coast of South Padre Island in the Gulf of Mexico. We had traveled together some distance in a caravan of cars and vans, and when we arrived, the weather was hot, sunny, and sultry—perfect for enjoying the beach and the ocean.

The head pastor and several adult chaperones were more familiar with this part of the country than I was. In fact, at that point in my life, it was the first time that I had ever seen an ocean.

The next day, during free time, I made a beeline straight for the beach. There was a perfect blue sky and the water was gorgeous. After goofing around with some of the kids in the water, I parted company from the crowd and set out for a good swim.

I had been a lifeguard and I had always been a strong swimmer, so I eagerly swam out beyond the breaking waves. Lost in the beauty of the moment, I rolled over onto my back and just floated, noticing every wisp of cloud that accented the sky and the seagulls overhead in their endless frolic. Feeling the caress of the warm sun on my body, I drifted off—literally. It was as though I had fallen into a meditative trance—and when I returned to my senses, I realized the current had carried me so far out to sea that the shoreline was barely discernible.

Although I suddenly realized that I had a long swim ahead of me, I was not concerned, for I knew I had the endurance to accomplish the distance without undue effort. I firmly told myself not to panic, to start swimming in the direction that most of the waves were heading. If I ended up on another part of the beach, I would simply walk back to my group. Getting to shore was the main objective.

I swam steadily back to shore, occasionally treading water to make sure of my bearings. Soon, thankfully, I was able to see the shore. But I knew that I was still fighting against a strong current that seemed just as determined to keep me out to sea as I was to reach the beach.

I was treading water to get my bearings again when something huge slammed against my legs.

Again something hit me with such force that I was swept off balance.

Another jolt and I was screaming for help.

My training as a lifeguard had taught me not to panic, but it was all that I could do to stay above water.

Whatever it was, it kept on whapping me, and I went under the waves several times. I kept attempting to swim toward shore, but I was being battered back to sea with every attempt.

Big fish was all that came to mind as I tried to make out what it was that was hitting me with such force. Or perhaps big fishes, for there seemed to be two kinds of skin hitting against me—one very rough, the other smooth.

At last I was near enough to shore so that someone heard my screams for help. I went under, came up, and saw a friend about ten feet away from me, trying to rescue me. Almost the instant I spotted him, a look of absolute terror came over his face.

I was going under for the third time. I couldn't get air. I couldn't swim. I just kept being hit. Then I passed out.

The next thing I knew I was in some wonderful stranger's strong arms, being lifted out of the water. As I came to, I saw that I was covered with blood from head to toe.

I was brought immediately to the first aid ranger station, where I interrupted a long line of people awaiting treatment. The ranger took one look at me in the arms of my rescuer and cleared the emergency table. I thought the man who was already on the table looked in worse condition than I: he had a sword from a stingray piercing his entire thigh.

The ranger looked me over carefully, wiping away the blood and examining the scraped areas. When his attention centered on my feet, he yelled to the other rangers in the first aid station, "Shark! Clear the beaches. Put out the shark alert signs. And get to the loudspeakers. Now!"

Then he turned to me and said, "My dear, you are one lucky woman to be alive."

I had been scraped from head to toe by the sandpaper-like skin of a shark, he explained. "And look at those shark teeth in your toes. Do you want them when I get them out?"

I declined the offer of the trophy. Later, I was transported to a hospital for shots and further examination. Then I was released and solemnly informed how fortunate I was.

When I arrived back at the camp where my teenagers had pitched their tents, my reception was less than enthusiastic. Of course everyone was thankful that I was safe, but, at the same time, they were disappointed by the news that the rangers had declared the beach off limits for several days because of my shark attack.

The rangers theorized that the monster had been taking its time, casually bumping up against me and nibbling at me, preparatory to making its final strike. However, before that fatal lunge could be made, something else in the water—something I was dimly aware of—had caused the shark to change its mind.

It took more than six months before I could wear a shoe on the foot where the ranger had pulled out the shark's teeth.

Later, as I was recounting the incident to some friends, I said that I had been aware of a couple of large marine bodies—other than the shark—in the water with me. One of the group who was listening to my dramatic account was a noted authority on dolphins. He stated emphatically that it was most likely dolphins that had saved me from the shark.

"Sherry, I believe your guardian angel was a dolphin," he said. "My research indicates that dolphins are among the few creatures that will take on a shark."

He went on to say that since sharks' teeth had been taken from my toes, the likelihood of the blood from the scrapes on my body and the bites on my feet drawing other sharks to the area was overwhelming. He continued to tell of a few examples in his work with dolphins in which a dolphin or a group of dolphins had moved in on a shark to ward off an attack.

I sensed instantly that he was correct. A dolphin had saved my life. I had always been thankful to God for the unnamed person who pulled me out of the water. But for me to have survived to that point, I believe that He had already sent an angel to protect me in the water.

Now I consider it likely that both of my rescuers— both in human and dolphin form—were my guardian angels that saved my life.

Sherry Hansen Steiger

When I was twelve years old and living in Texas, I was wild about horses and enjoyed riding them. It was a special thrill when my grandmother on my father's side, Grandmother Loden, gave me a beautiful, retired quarter horse racer. I decided to call her Cinnamon because of her lovely reddish color.

I was always eager to go out to Grandmother Loden's farm after school and on weekends to ride Cinnamon. I had always wanted a horse to call my own.

However, I quickly learned that Cinnamon did not especially share my enthusiasm for riding or return my affection. Perhaps Cinnamon felt that because she was retired from racing, she didn't really care to have a young girl bouncing around on her back and making her work up a sweat. I also soon discovered that Cinnamon had a bit of an attitude and was quite independent—but I felt that for the most part we got along very well, and I believed that everything would work out all right.

Cinnamon's stubborn streak would express itself most strongly when I would ride her out to the far pasture's end, which was bordered by an irrigation ditch that supplied water to various farms. It was at this point that I would turn her around and plan to race back at high speed.

But no! Each time, Cinnamon would kneel down as if she were a camel and would refuse to get up until I removed the saddle from her back.

Then she would get up, whinny and squeal in delight, and race back to the barn—leaving me to walk all the way back, carrying and dragging the heavy western saddle for nearly a mile.

After lugging the big saddle back to the barn all by myself a few times, I began to figure that maybe she had a point. There was no question that a racing saddle wasn't nearly as heavy as a western range saddle.

On one or two occasions, I had ridden Cinnamon bareback, without any saddle at all, and I had truly enjoyed riding her in that style. As I held tightly to her mane to keep from falling off her back, it seemed to me that she was trying to outrace the Texas summer breezes that accompanied us on many of our rides.

Uncle Joe, my dad's brother, told me that Cinnamon would eventually get used to the heavier saddle and realize that she was not a race horse any longer, so I should just be patient. I also realized that Grandmother Loden had especially picked out the saddle to go with the horse, and it was truly beautiful, with its deeply carved leather and its lovely pattern of silver inlay.

On my next two or three rides with Cinnamon, I was seated in the handsome saddle atop her back and everything went smoothly. Of course, it might have been because Uncle Joe accompanied us on his horse.

A week later when I saddled Cinnamon, she seemed eager to start out, even though I had a strange, uneasy feeling. As we began our ride, it seemed as if she were flying across the pasture—but all too soon we approached the section that bordered the irrigation ditch. I noticed that the water was overflowing the rim of the ditch at the same moment that Cinnamon did her camel routine, kneeling down right in the mud and refusing to get up.

I was so upset. I had hoped that we had moved beyond this tiresome bit.

I pleaded with her to get back up, and I tugged at the reins to help and encourage her to get back on all four feet.

But she only shook her head, squealing to let me know that she had no intention of getting up until the heavy western saddle was *off her back*!

Because the irrigation ditch was overflowing its banks, I was splashing about in the mud. It seemed that she had deliberately chosen to kneel where both of us would get really dirty.

And the way the stirrups had bunched up . . . it was going to be very difficult and awkward getting the saddle off this temperamental horse who was choosing to kneel stubbornly in the mud.

As I tugged and pulled at the saddle, I became more upset with Cinnamon by the moment.

And I was disgusted with myself for wanting to believe so desperately that everything was just great—

even though I had felt from the start that it was going to be a strange day. But oh, no, I had refused to listen to my inner voice. I vowed that I would never, never ignore it again.

I was so upset that I was crying by the time I was in the final process of removing the saddle.

Cinnamon suddenly jumped to her feet, and before I had completed lifting the heavy western saddle off her back, she shook herself to free her coat of any loose mud that she had acquired from kneeling in the soupy overflow from the irrigation ditch. Her sudden, violent muscular movements sent both the loosened saddle and me into a mud puddle.

The saddle landed on my legs and momentarily pinned me under its weight. Thankfully, my western boots protected a portion of my legs from getting bruised by the heavy saddle as I lay there, mad and muddy.

Cinnamon trotted about fifteen feet away and stood observing me. Well, at least this time it appeared that she wasn't going to race off and leave me to walk back alone.

But neither did she make any movement to return to me to have the saddle replaced on her back.

So there was nothing else for me to do but to wait a few minutes, catch my breath, then get up, hoist the saddle to my shoulder, and start walking back to the barn.

Suddenly Cinnamon squealed again, but this time there was an edge of fright to her whinny. She reared up on her hind legs and began to paw the air.

I was startled. I had never seen her act like that. As much as we had disagreed about the western saddle, she was not a mean horse. She was really very nice — and up to that moment, I had never considered her anything other than high-spirited.

And then I looked a bit to the right and straight ahead. Cinnamon had reared because a huge water moccasin had crossed right in front of her and was headed directly toward me.

My heart began pounding in my chest. I still lay sprawled in the mud, tangled up in the saddle, which was on top of my legs, restricting my movement.

The snake glided to within three or four feet of me — and stopped to begin its coil.

I didn't want to believe what I was seeing. I broke out in a cold sweat. I knew that water moccasins were very poisonous and were relatives to the copperheads. But unlike the common Texas rattlesnakes, they do not give warning of their nasty intentions.

This one was really big, and it had unusual spots on it. Its body was about the size of a healthy fence post.

In my twelve-year-old's instinct for survival, it seemed the best thing for me to do was to holler for help. So I began to do just that — though I had no idea who could hear me and who could possibly come to my rescue before that huge snake completed its coil and struck out to sink its fangs into the nearest portion of my body.

Cinnamon, however, had already started a plan of attack.

I'll never forget what happened in those next few moments. Rather than running from the big snake, she came galloping toward me just as the snake was finishing its coil.

Instantly she whirled around and with her back legs kicked at the snake.

Miraculously, her hooves struck the snake with such impact that it looked like a weird football that had been kicked for a field goal as it sailed into the air. Then, coming out of its coil, it fell with a huge "kersplash" into the water of the irrigation ditch.

Cinnamon came running over to me, quivering with excess energy, but starting to calm down some. She, too, knew that the danger was gone.

I couldn't believe it. Stubborn old Cinnamon, with her attitude and all, had just saved me from a horrible fate.

At about that time Uncle Joe rode into sight. He had spotted the ruckus from the next pasture, and he rounded the corner just as the snake was sailing in the air.

As we started back to the barn, Uncle Joe smiled when I said that I wanted to give Cinnamon a special reward for saving my life. I said that I would never again make her wear a heavy western saddle. And she never did!

Clarisa Bernhardt,
Internationally known Psychic

*M*any might say our little Pleiades is a pampered pet. Gael carries Pleiades in her own special little basket, and feels that she is a very special being who just happens presently to reside in a little dog's body. She has such a charming personality that she spreads joy and laughter everywhere she goes.

Gael explains: Interestingly, I raised Pleiades to be a vegetarian, and although it's unusual for a dog, her very favorite food is snow peas! She is so small that I have to take each pea out of the pod and feed them to her one at a time, and even one little pea is a mouthful for her. Whenever possible, I make sure that her peas are always fresh and organic.

In the local market near where I live in Flagstaff, Arizona, the checkout people all know Pleiades and her love for snow peas. They are used to her barking at the cashier as if to say, "Be sure my snow peas are first!" They are usually very careful to see that the snow peas are checked from the shopping basket first thing. If they should forget, Pleiades will bark so loud she is sure to be heard in the next two checkout counters. Everyone around seems to delight in this unique tiny dog's eagerness and excitement over his treat, and all in earshot of this snow pea ritual get a good laugh.

My special love and attention for my tiny little friend is always rewarded with the unending love she gives back to me; but I had no idea that she was soon to save my life and that of my husband, Patrick.

We live in a gorgeous area near Sedona, in Flagstaff, Arizona, where there are many mountains and some dangerous curves for drivers. We were on our way home one day, when all of a sudden Pleiades began acting very strange. She stood up in her little basket and started making some weird sounds. Patrick and I were so surprised at her unusual behavior that we slowed down to see what was the matter with her.

We pulled over to the side of the road as far as possible and examined Pleiades, but we were not able to spot anything visibly wrong with her, so we decided to start up again.

As we slowly pulled into the lane we noticed that we were just approaching the blind curve of a narrow mountain road. On the other side of the curve was a hundred-foot drop. We deliberately slowed down around this curve—and were shocked to see a vehicle stretched across the road broadside, filling both lanes. It seems that a tourist had chosen this spot to make a nearly impossible U-turn in the center of the highway, and there he was sitting, as we rounded the bend.

If it had not been for Pleiades, we would not have been able to stop and quite possibly we would have all gone down the hill. We certainly would have broad-sided the car sitting there, and one or both cars would have had no place else to go but down.

We are sure Pleiades must have been able to sense that something was not right. She certainly was trying to warn us of the unseen danger that was just ahead. We now know what was wrong with her—she was trying to save our lives!

If it had not been for Pleiades, we might not be here now, so needless to say we are so thankful for her alert behavior. Patrick and I both hugged and kissed our little friend, and we bought her five pounds of fresh snow peas that night!

Patrick Flanagan
Gael Crystal Flanagan

I've thought a lot about my story, and I have tried very hard to explain it in terms that would make sense to a rational, scientifically minded man or woman. Maybe I can, but probably I can't.

I was only thirteen when the incident occurred. I was baby-sitting for Mrs. Kirkland's twin girls, Naomi and Natalie, who were four at that time. I was pretty tall for my age, and I looked older than I really was, so Mrs. Kirkland trusted me to take the girls walking in the woods and around the lake in the northern Wisconsin area where we lived.

My mom, though, would always admonish me to be careful with those little girls and would lecture me about the responsibility of caring for other people's children. She was a schoolteacher, so I guess both lecturing people and looking out for other people's kids came naturally to her.

On this particular crisp fall day, I had bundled the girls up in nice, warm coats, and I promised them each a piece of licorice if they didn't fuss or complain about anything. Naomi, especially, was kind of a fussbudget and would whine and cry about nothing. Then when Mrs. Kirkland would come home and see tear stains on the girl's cheeks, she would give me a kind of fish-eye, as if maybe I was being mean to the girls. Since Natalie was always giggling and laughing, I guess things kind of balanced out.

I didn't pay a whole lot of attention to the car that pulled into the lane behind us when we were about to cut across the Jensens' field to walk over to a pond. I did notice that it had an out-of-state license plate. Illinois. But it wasn't out of the ordinary at that time of year to have a lot of Illinois cars driving up to see the changing of the leaves.

When I heard the car doors shut, though, I turned to see just who would be getting out in this lonely place and what they would be intending to do.

I saw a burly looking man about my dad's age. He looked really scruffy. It looked like he hadn't shaved for days, and he had a thick, dark beard.

Somehow I got a sudden flash that he was after the twins.

I had heard my mom and dad talking about a ring of babynappers who stole kids from their parents and sold them in some kind of elaborate black market in the big cities. Pretty little blonde girls like Natalie and Naomi would probably be real prizes.

I tried to hurry the girls along. The man was kind of fat, so I figured we could easily outdistance him and get to the Jensens' farmhouse before he could catch us.

I had no idea that a big man could run so fast. He was up on us in no time.

I picked up a stick and waved it like a baseball bat. "You stay away, mister," I warned him. "You go back to your car. Leave us alone!"

He called me a "feisty little something or other" and laughed at me. He said we could do it the easy way or the hard way. The easy way was if I just ran away and let him take the girls without any fuss. The hard way was if he had to waste time by stopping to break my neck.

Naomi had started whining and sobbing the minute the man had run up to us. When he made a grab for the girls, Natalie let out a scream like I had never heard come from her lips.

And then, just like that, there must have been twenty or thirty sparrows and a couple of blackbirds swooping down on him. They were all squawking and pecking and scratching at him as if they meant to do him in permanently.

It all happened so suddenly that he was thrown off balance and fell to the ground. He started yelling and crying and cursing. He would try to get up and swing at the birds, but it was like someone trying to hit the wind. They just moved higher and swooped down harder.

I picked up both of the girls, kind of balancing them on my hips and holding one with each arm, and I ran as fast as I could with that kind of load straight to the Jensens' farmhouse. Luckily, Mrs. Jensen was home, and she called the sheriff just as soon as I told her what had happened.

Of course the kidnapper had gotten away long before the sheriff and his deputy got there. They found a lot of blood drops splattered in the grass where he had thrashed around on the ground. When they asked me what had happened there, I told them about the big swarm of birds descending from the skies to attack him.

A lot of folks where I grew up are pretty religious. I remember the deputy talking about "avenging angels from the skies on high."

Ingrid P.

*J*ohn and Cassandra Kraven had not wanted to bring their cat along with them during their summer vacation in the Adirondack Mountains, fearing that it would be too much bother. But when a friend who had promised to kitty-sit had been called out of town at the last minute, they had no choice but to bring Jasper along.

"Look at it this way," Cassandra said, making the best of the situation. "Jasper will help keep Janie from getting bored."

John wondered how their daughter could possibly become bored surrounded by the breathtaking beauty of the Adirondacks in the lovely cottage they had rented for two weeks.

"Well, dear," Cassandra gently reminded him, "two-year-old girls might not appreciate the wonder of the great outdoors without television and cartoon shows."

The first few days at the cottage had been truly relaxing for the Kravens, and little Janie had enjoyed the walks in the woods and the storytelling around the fireplace at night. Jasper found a hundred different items of interest to appease his cat's curiosity and proved to be no bother at all.

On the fourth day of their vacation, however, Jasper would prove to be a hero of Olympian stature.

John and Cassandra were reading in comfortable lawn chairs on the front porch, and Janie was playing in a clump of wildflowers just a few yards from the cottage. Suddenly, without any warning, a large black bear lumbered into the yard.

Before either John or Cassandra could respond to the situation in any manner whatsoever, the huge animal had grabbed their daughter and was shaking her in his snout as if she were a rag doll.

The terrified parents were paralyzed in a freeze frame of total shock as they beheld the ultimate horror of their daughter in the jaws of a marauding monster.

At that moment of primeval terror, Jasper leaped onto the bear's head, fastened his back claws into its flesh, and scratched at the brute's eyes until it dropped Janie in order to better direct its wrath at the enraged cat.

Jasper, seeing Janie now released from the behemoth's jaws, jumped to the ground, deftly avoiding the clumsy giant's swiping paws. Then, with the angry bear in hot pursuit, Jasper raced off into the forest.

John and Cassandra ran to their daughter, who, though crying in fear, seemed unharmed. Miraculously, the bear's huge teeth had snatched at the girl's playsuit and had not punctured her flesh.

If it hadn't been for Jasper's dramatic intervention, however, they could not even bring themselves to think of what might have happened to their precious Janie.

After about two hours, Jasper returned in triumph to the cabin, completely unharmed. The Kravens theorized that their courageous kitty had led the bear on a merry chase deep in the forest, thus luring him far away from their cottage.

Cassandra and John know that they owe their daughter's life to Jasper, the cat they thought would be too much bother to bring along on their vacation. They have, in fact, stated solemnly that they will never again travel far out of town without being accompanied by their fierce attack cat.

*O*ne day in May of 1995, my wife Lauren and I decided that it was a perfect afternoon to take Lara, our three-year-old daughter, to a nearby park in the northern California community in which we have lived for the past four years.

Walking along the sidewalk on a busy two-lane street and pushing Lara in a stroller, we were suddenly joined by a large dog of mixed breed that Lauren and I jokingly decided seemed "mostly Labrador." The poor thing was very thin, and its sandy-colored hair was matted and dirty. I noticed that it wasn't wearing a collar, and I became somewhat nervous when it continued to follow us down the street.

"Watch that Lara doesn't get too close to the dog," I told Lauren.

Lauren shrugged. "Why? It seems friendly enough."

I explained that it had no collar so it was obviously a stray. That meant that friendly or not, the mutt could possibly have distemper or some other disease. "And you don't know where that mouth has been," I added for emphasis. "You don't want a tongue that has just dined on garbage licking Lara in the face."

Lauren made a distorted face of distaste and bent over to wave her hand at the dog and tell him to get away.

While we were momentarily distracted by our efforts to chase the dog away from Lara, she had spotted a balloon vendor in a clown suit standing across the street at the entrance to the park. Excited by the funny man and the colorful balloons, she already had one leg out of the stroller before we noticed what she was doing.

As if in a nightmare, Lauren and I actually bumped into each other as we lunged for Lara. While we tottered to regain our footing, she ran right into the street behind a parked car.

The nightmarish sensation intensified when we saw that a large green van was speeding down the road toward us. We knew that he would be unable to see Lara because of the parked car.

Lauren screamed in terror, and I started to run for Lara, my heart pounding, but I knew that there was no way I could reach her in time.

And now the nightmare scenario had become all too real. We were about to see our only child die before our eyes.

That was when the stray mutt dashed past me and somehow got in front of Lara. Then, in a maneuver that seemed practiced, he twisted his body and knocked her backwards and out of the path of the van. And while it appeared for an instant that the dog himself would be struck, he managed a graceful turn that spun him out of danger.

My whole body felt numb as I picked Lara off the street and set her back in her stroller. All three of us were shaking and crying and hugging, and Lauren and I were giving God our thanks for working a miracle through the agency of this wonderful dog.

And then Lauren and I were on our knees hugging, petting, and thanking the stray mutt that had entered our lives just in time to save our daughter's life. He licked both of us on our cheeks and hands, but we never gave a thought where that tongue might have been or on what it might have dined.

The dog continued to follow us into the park, keeping close beside us. "I think he believes he has found a home," I said, chuckling at the way Lara kept reaching over to pet him as he kept pace with her stroller.

Lauren nodded and smiled. "No dog in history ever earned a home more than this fellow just did."

We held hands, and I could feel that she was still shaking over the close call with Lara and the speeding van.

"We'll call him Ira," I said. "That's Hebrew for 'he who watches.' If our four-legged friend hadn't been watching over Lara, we would have lost our beloved little daughter."

"Ira it is," Lauren agreed.

And then we stopped at a concession stand before walking home and bought hamburgers for everyone. Actually, three for Ira. Now that he had a home with us, we would be certain to put some meat on those bones.

Leonard J.

O*ne* night, I was awakened from a sound sleep by a tremendous crashing noise in my apartment. Startled, I cautiously proceeded to get out of bed and search for the source of the noise.

As I made my way to the hall I saw that my frequent fears of an intruder in my apartment had finally been realized. There in the hall was a man holding a gun — and he was aiming it at me, telling me to get the hell back to my bedroom.

I knew it would not be a good idea to do anything other than comply immediately with the intruder's demand. I had started to back up to return to my bedroom, when like a speeding bullet, my cat, Nicky, shot past me, hissing and growling.

Nicky was so much a "love rag" cat that the sight of my gentle pet transforming himself into an "attack cat" was astounding to me. But attack he did. Nicky had flown into such a monsterlike rage, jumping on and attacking the would-be assailant — gun and all — that the burglar turned and ran out the front door of my apartment.

Still in a slight panic myself, I locked the front door instantly, and walked around the rest of my apartment. It was then that I discovered that the burglar had come in through a window. He had gone to some effort to get in through the bars that had been put on the window to keep intruders out. Somehow, he had managed to bend the bars and squeeze in between them.

My ferocious cat Nicky scared the thief so badly that he didn't even take the time to back out through the point of entry, but instead chose to exit the fastest way possible—through the front door! So don't let anyone tell you it isn't possible for a cat to be a protector and defender. I always used to laugh at those funny signs that say, "Beware, Watch Cat"—but now I think I had better get one. My watch cat certainly defended me and most likely saved my life! He certainly deserves the title.

Michael Talbot, author of
The Holographic Universe

*M*y husband Byron and I were both born in the Dallas–Fort Worth area and lived in that urban enclave all of our lives—until we moved to the country in Oklahoma just a few years ago.

I have a phobia about snakes, particularly rattlesnakes. The first year we were in our new rural home, we didn't have any trouble with snakes. I believe the reason was that shortly after we moved to the country, I went out into the yard and sat talking silently to the snakes and rodents, explaining that they were not welcome in our yard or in our home. After all, I pointed out, they had fifteen thousand acres of state game preserve directly behind us and a thousand acres of natural habitat all around us. They had plenty of space in which to make their homes and to live in peace without interfering in our habitat.

But then, the first winter we lived there, eight hundred acres were logged across the road. This upset the natural habitat of many of the animals, including the snakes. In short order, we had a problem with rattlesnakes and other crawling creatures coming into the yard.

Thankfully, that was when we were presented with the gift of a black Labrador retriever named Jake, a beautiful dog with a special talent for sniffing out rattlesnakes. And we soon learned that Jake had a special bark that he sounded whenever he spotted a rattler. It is a loud, shrill bark that is completely different from his usual bark. Whenever we hear it, we know that Jake has cornered a rattlesnake. He will run around the snake, containing it in one place, until Byron comes to dispose of it.

I have no fear of rattlesnakes now. I feel that Jake has saved us from serious bites and saved me from suffering great frights. Especially since once he cornered a cottonmouth in the carport, right near the back door to our house.

One day in the fall of 1997, Jake ran into the woods as usual, but didn't return for three days. All the while, I prayed that he would return to us unharmed, for there are many large and dangerous predators in the woods.

Jake came back with his hind leg almost denuded of all fur. His leg was red and raw, with the muscle showing. When our neighbors saw the injuries that he had suffered, they all sadly agreed that Jake would not live much longer. They wondered how he had managed to survive as long as he had.

I prayed and talked to Jake. I told him that I needed him to take care of me and to protect me from the many rattlesnakes that live all around us.

It took several weeks for his injuries to begin to heal, but today, after many months, Jake's hind leg is once again covered with fur and he has full use of it. I feel that his knowing how much I depended on him to alert us to rattlesnakes was an instrumental factor in his healing. Jake is back to his usual self, running once again in the woods, keeping a vigil for rattlesnakes.

Jake is not as handsome as he once was, but to me he is more beautiful than any of our other dogs. He is special, no doubt about it. He is my dog angel.

Annie Kirkwood, author of
Mary's Message to the World

*P*igs suffer from inaccurate stereotypes, centuries old, that portray them as dirty, stupid, lazy animals. In truth, they are only as dirty as their environment demands, and they are clean enough to be considered ideal house pets by some contented pig owners. And when it comes to a survey of the IQs of barnyard animals, the pig will quite likely be found to score near the top for native intelligence. As for the charge of being a lazy critter . . .

In 1995, Priscilla, a three-month-old pig, became the first animal inducted into the Texas Veterinary Medical Association's Pet Hall of Fame when she saved an eleven-year-old boy from drowning.

Priscilla had been swimming with her owner in a Houston lake when she heard the frightened cries of Anthony Melton, who had panicked and begun to drown. The little pig responded at once and began to paddle toward the screaming boy.

Once she was next to him, Priscilla nudged Anthony with her snout, grunting and signaling for him to grab on to her harness.

Perhaps it was the extraordinary circumstances of a paddling pig bobbing next to him that punctured the boy's panic and allowed him to focus on the animal's obvious pantomimed communication. He reached out to grab hold of the pig's harness, and Priscilla towed him straight to the safety of the shore.

Seventy-three-year-old James Gudmonson, a farmer in northwest Iowa, was driving his tractor around a drainage ditch to check on the water level in the creek that ran through his place when suddenly the tractor overturned.

Although it happened so quickly, Jim remembered being pinned between the front and rear wheels — and then the tractor overturned twice more, knocking him unconscious.

When he regained consciousness and his mind cleared, he was flat on his back, pinned beneath the tractor, with a broken leg. He tried to move and free himself, but he soon discovered that he was unable to escape from either the weight of the tractor or the terrible pain that came from his broken limb.

Dang it all, he told himself, he was too darned old to be still farming. He should have retired. He should have left the farming to his son Arnie. If he had, he winced, as tears of pain and frustration stung his eyes, he wouldn't be in this mess right now.

A few minutes later, when he tried to sit up, he saw Brenda, his grandson Jerry's two-year-old German shepherd, watching him from about twenty feet away. The dog must have followed him into the field, hoping for some excitement to break the monotony of watching the pigs and cattle chew their feed.

Ha! She sure got her wish, all right! But Jim was sorry that the mutt was getting this much excitement. Jim could easily have done without tipping the tractor and pinning himself underneath just to entertain a dog.

Brenda! He had complained from the beginning that Brenda was a ridiculous name for a dog.

Brenda was a person's name, a girl's name. Female dogs should be named something like Queen or Princess or Lady or . . . well, something more suitable. Dogs were not supposed to have people names.

But eleven-year-old Jerry stubbornly said that he wanted a "real" name for his dog. He didn't want to call her Queen or Lady or anything of the sort. In his mind, the German shepherd was a person. And Brenda Gudmonson sounded like a real name.

In spite of his pain, Jim laughed at the dog with a "real" name as she slowly began to approach the scene of the accident. She had never been much good for anything. She had never been his idea of a real farm dog. She was as out of place on the farm as her name was on a dog.

Brenda came closer, sniffing around the tractor.

"That's right, you silly, brainless dog," Jim said, clenching his teeth against the pain. "The tractor tipped over. See me pinned underneath? Now, if you were Lassie or Rin Tin Tin, I could send you for help. Fat chance I have with you!"

Jim wondered about his chances of getting help in time. He worried that he might have other injuries, internal ones, far more serious than a broken leg.

Arnie, his son, was in town at the farmers' elevator, delivering a truckload of corn to sell. Depending on how many trucks were ahead of him, Arnie could be gone a long time.

Ruth, his daughter-in-law, taught school and wouldn't be home for hours.

And, of course, Jerry, his grandson, was in school.

That left his seventy-year-old wife, Kay, who was terribly crippled with arthritis, and Brenda, the wonder dog, to help him.

Jim lapsed into unconsciousness once again, and in a kind of dream state, he saw Brenda rushing home and alerting Kay to his predicament. Somehow comprehending the significance of every bark and whine, Kay called the neighbors, and Lonny Hankins came to rescue him with his four-wheel-drive truck.

When Jim opened his eyes, he saw that Brenda was chewing at the denim jacket that he had draped around the tractor seat.

Worthless dog! She probably smelled the sandwich wrapper that he had stuffed in a jacket pocket after his lunch.

"Fine help you are!" Jim said angrily. "That's all you ever think about. Filling your belly and sleeping."

Brenda pulled at the jacket pocket until a large piece of it ripped away.

"Selfish, greedy dog!" Jim shouted.

Brenda ran off with the cloth in her mouth. The last sight Jim had of her was when she turned away from the scene of the accident, padded downhill, and disappeared into the woods around the creek.

"Good riddance, you good-for-nothing!" Jim yelled after her.

He tried with all of his strength to pull his leg free of the tractor. Then he mercifully lapsed into unconsciousness.

When he opened his eyes, Brenda was licking his cheek and he was looking into the concerned faces of his wife Kay and his neighbor Lonny Hankins.

"I knew right away that something was wrong when Brenda came pawing at the kitchen door, all wet and muddy from the creek," Kay told him. "She dropped a piece of denim from your jacket from between her jaws, then started barking till all get-out. I just knew right away that something must have happened to you."

Kay had immediately called the neighbors and told them that Jim needed help.

"Old Brenda saved your bacon, Jim," Lonny told him.

In spite of his pain, Jim felt sheepish and ashamed as he told Brenda what a good dog she was.

"You just sit tight, Jim," Lonny said, "and we'll have you out of there in no time."

"Don't worry. I'll wait right here until you get me loose," Jim answered before he passed out again.

When the doctors examined him at the hospital, they found that Jim Gudmonson had suffered a broken pelvis, cracked ribs, and internal injuries in addition to the broken leg. If he had lain there much longer, according to the attending physician, he might not have lived.

Weeks later, when Jim was able to return to the farm, he told his grandson Jerry and the German shepherd at his side that Brenda was a fine name for a dog. A really smart dog that had saved his life.

*I*n Galveston, Texas, Skipper is known as the cat with the three-million-dollar meow. After centuries of folktales about such magical cats as "Puss in Boots," who brings a fortune to his young master, the fairy tale finally came true in the winter of 1996.

Linda and Gayle McManamon were relaxing at home watching television, only dimly aware that Skipper, their cat, was playing around on the floor with a lottery shaker—a simple device that some people use to help choose numbers.

When Gayle glanced down to smile at Skipper's idle play, he suddenly became aware that the cat had picked six numbers—8, 11, 16, 25, 26, and 42. Either on a whim or on guidance from some higher power, Gayle decided to write the numbers down on a slip of paper.

The next day when Linda was preparing to go to the store to purchase their weekly lottery tickets, Gayle told her to play the numbers that Skipper had picked.

Incredibly, that night all six numbers were drawn.

But Linda and Gayle didn't discover that their ship had come in until the following day. Linda was at work when someone informed her that the lottery had been won by a ticket bought in Galveston.

By the time she talked to Gayle, he had known for about thirty minutes and had been temporarily transformed into a blubbering idiot. They had overnight become $3.72 million dollars richer.

The McManamons have said that they plan to turn over the family business to their son, open a day-care center for working mothers, and treat the cat with the three-million-dollar meow like a king for the rest of his life.

*S*eventy-five-year-old Jack Fyfe's terrible nightmare began when he awakened to find the left side of his body completely lacking all sensation. He felt as though a comet had crashed through the roof of his home in Sydney, Australia, and pinned him to his bed.

As he collected his thoughts, he realized that he must have had a stroke while he was sleeping.

With a supreme effort of will he attempted to roll out of bed, hoping that he might be able to drag himself to the telephone and call his daughter for help.

But he was completely unable to move.

That was when the horror of his predicament truly struck him full force. A widower, he lived alone with Trixie, his six-year-old Australian kelpie-border collie mix, and he was not expecting any visitors.

His daughter had invited him to a social event, but that was nine days away. A virtual recluse like himself would be unlikely to be missed in those nine days.

Jack did his best to fight back the panic that had begun to permeate every corner of his mind. Finally, he began to scream, even though his cries for help were barely more than useless whispers.

Only Trixie, whining at his bedside in canine sympathy, heard his agonized pleas for assistance.

It was very hot in the house. Jack knew it had to be over ninety degrees. He was very likely to die a slow, torturous death of thirst long before anyone missed him.

After a few hours, he pitifully cried out for water as he drifted in and out of consciousness. Each time he would once again become aware of his predicament, he would laugh bitterly at his plight. Why cry for water when there was no one there to bring it to him?

Yes, but there was someone there who heard his hoarse cries and who understood that her master very desperately needed something to drink.

Trixie suddenly left the bedroom and went into the kitchen. Jack could hear her lapping water from her bowl.

"Ahh, Trixie," he sighed, "if only you could bring me a drink."

And that was precisely what Trixie did.

Oh, perhaps it wasn't the most sanitary of methods — but who would worry about such petty concerns when he was dying of thirst? Trixie jumped up on Jack's bed and released a snoutful of water into his mouth.

Jack later recalled that the sensation of the water reaching his parched lips and throat was wonderful. He had often repeated the word *water* as he filled Trixie's bowl, but for her to interpret his feeble gasping of the word as a request for her to fetch water and deliver it mouth-to-mouth seemed a miracle.

For days, each time Jack would call out for water, Trixie heeded his request.

When her water bowl ran dry, the resourceful dog got a towel and dipped it in the toilet bowl.

Jack had no qualms about where the life-preserving water was obtained. He thankfully sucked on the soaked towel as if he were a helpless baby.

For nine days, Trixie kept Jack Fyfe alive until he at last heard his daughter at the front door. From time to time, his telephone had rung, and he had assumed that it was his daughter calling to discuss plans for the social event that they were to attend. He had prayed that she would soon become concerned because he never answered the telephone. And now she was there— and she had brought paramedics along with her. He was saved.

Jack's daughter and his attending physician were astonished to learn how the faithful Trixie had kept her master alive those nine awful days. And Jack Fyfe himself rested more comfortably in the hospital knowing that he had a most remarkable friend awaiting him back home.

*I*n July of 1996, Martin Richardson, a twenty-nine-year-old adventurer from Colchester, England, left the diving boat he was sailing in when he spotted three bottlenose dolphins in the Red Sea off Egypt's Sinai Peninsula. He thought it would be wonderful to join them and play with them in the water, but they disappeared when he entered the sea.

He was floating on his back and relaxing in the warm waters when a great white shark suddenly emerged from the sea and clamped its monstrous jaws around his shoulder.

That very first bite punctured a lung and tore away part of a rib and some muscle.

Richardson tried to swim for the diving boat and he shouted for help, but his friends were over a hundred yards away.

Within a few seconds, the monster struck at his left side, once again tearing away flesh with its massive jaws.

Richardson did not wish his final resting place to be in the belly of the ugly brute. He punched down on the shark's head and nose as hard as he could, and once again the sea beast released him.

Reeling from shock, Richardson did his best to swim away from all the blood in the water that had poured from his terrible wounds, but the vicious predator tore into him a third time.

Somehow, even though the third strike had ripped away even more flesh and exposed Richardson's spine, the Englishman, fighting desperately for his survival, managed to punch the shark away once again.

But seconds later, the hideous, beady-eyed monster was on him again, chewing flesh from his chest.

It was at that awful moment, Richardson said, that he prayed to God for a miracle. He shouted to the heavens that he had never before asked for very much, but now his life was in His hands.

Richardson knew the next strike from the great white would finish him off. The pain was beyond anything that he could imagine, and he was so weak that he could barely stay afloat.

And then God answered his plea for a miracle by sending the three bottlenose dolphins that had first attracted Richardson into the warm waters of the Red Sea.

The dolphins formed a protective ring around him and beat the water with their tails and fins in order to frighten the shark away from its prey. And they continued their defensive tactic until Richardson's friends in the diving boat were able to pull alongside him in an inflatable boat.

The Recanati Center for Maritime Studies at the University of Haifa in Israel stated that such a defensive measure by dolphins is common when they are protecting their young from predators.

Associated Press reports said that doctors at the hospital in el-Tur, Egypt, placed two hundred stitches in Richardson's left shoulder, stomach, and back. Attending physicians told him that he had lost eleven pounds of flesh to the Great White and that he could anticipate a hospital stay of at least a week. Miraculously, the doctors informed him that their prognosis suggested that he would experience a full recovery.

Later, when they measured the teeth marks on his body, it was estimated that the beast had a jaw span of nearly two feet and was probably about fourteen feet long.

Richardson told the media that he had always loved dolphins—and now he owed his life to them.

In the early 1970s, Bob Holborn, a plumber turned deep-sea diver, trained "Beaky," a Cornish dolphin, to become an accomplished lifeguard. According to writer Dennis Bardens, the amiable sea mammal was responsible for saving many lives in the waters off Land's End in Cornwall, England.

Holborn tells of the time when a sailor fell off the side of a boat and Beaky held him up in the water for several hours until help finally arrived.

On another occasion, one of Holborn's friends was diving off Land's End when a sudden thick fog separated him from his boat. Beaky saved his life by actually guiding the man to the steps of his diving boat.

On April 20, 1976, an accomplished diver named Keith Monery found himself in a desperate situation off Penzance, Cornwall. He had removed his life jacket after it had become filled with water and he had discarded his fifteen-pound weight belt, but he was still having great difficulty reaching the surface.

The sea had become rough, and Monery was rapidly nearing exhaustion. Although a friend had spotted the diver's distress signal—a clenched fist waved frantically to and fro—and had entered the water to attempt a rescue, another "friend" was much quicker.

Beaky streaked past the human rescuer, then got underneath the exhausted Monery and kept pushing him upward until he reached the surface and could be rescued.

*T*he doctors were not optimistic, and their words were far from encouraging. John and Sheila Morrison were informed that Rachel, their eleven-year-old daughter, had suffered severe brain damage. The tragic bottom line was that she might not live. And if she did, the medical experts warned, she might be a vegetable for the rest of her life.

The Morrisons were grief-stricken. What had begun as a pleasant outing on Labor Day, 1992, at an amusement park in Grand Prairie, Texas, had ended in tragedy.

They had decided to treat their pretty daughter to a roller-coaster ride. Then, as the car in which they were riding whipped around a bend, Rachel was thrown out. In horror, John and Sheila watched helplessly as she plummeted twenty-five feet to the ground below.

On October 7, desperate to explore any therapy that might restore their comatose daughter to their family, the Morrisons brought Rachel to the Baylor Institute for Rehabilitation in Dallas. The director of the program, Shari Bernard, understood that the eleven-year-old girl had been in a coma for five weeks, but she brought a number of dogs to Rachel's side and allowed them to approach her. To everyone's joy, she slowly began responding to a few simple commands given by Ms. Bernard.

Although they strove to remain positive at the first signs of any kind of breakthrough, realistically it was sadly apparent that the child's responses were scarcely more than robotlike movements; she still gave little evidence that she was truly in touch with her environment.

As the days passed, Rachel most often would simply sit still in her wheelchair, mute and unresponsive.

Then, on October 14, Ms. Bernard brought Belle, a lively Australian sheepdog, to Rachel's side. Later, she told reporter Philip Smith how the girl slowly reached out to put her arm over the dog.

"Australian sheepdogs have no tails," Shari Bernard told Rachel. Then she asked Rachel directly what Belle was missing.

Without hesitation, Rachel whispered, "A tail."

Those were the first words that the girl had spoken since her terrible fall on Labor Day six weeks ago.

Ms. Bernard admitted that she had been stunned. It was as if Belle had somehow been able to penetrate the deep recesses of the child's consciousness and enable her to speak again.

That evening, to Sheila Morrison's unrestrained joy, she was able to speak to Rachel on the telephone.

Later, in discussing the case of Rachel Morrison, Shari Bernard said that in the eight years that she had worked in pet therapy at the Baylor Institute for Rehabilitation, she had never witnessed a case quite so dramatic as that of the comatose eleven-year-old who spoke after connecting with a dog. She said that it seemed as though there was a special bond between the two.

Rachel, who continued to make steady progress after her dramatic breakthrough, simply commented that she loved being with dogs and that there was something about Belle that made her want to speak again.

*B*ack in the 1930s when electricity was still new on the farm, a neighbor of mine constructed a homemade electric fence by using 220-volt direct current, which packed quite a wallop.

One day my five-year-old brother and an uncle were walking in an Oregon rain with our pet bulldog, Sarge. My brother, being an inquisitive child, decided to see if the wire of the electric fence would really shock a person in the rain. Again, being a typical boy, he had walked through every mud puddle, thoroughly soaking his feet, thus providing electricity with excellent grounding.

Needless to say, my brother got severely shocked—to the point where he could not let go.

When my uncle saw what had occurred and tried to release him, he found that the two of them were "frozen" together by the charge of the high-voltage electricity. They would both surely have died within minutes.

Somehow, Sarge perceived the trouble in which my little brother and my uncle had placed themselves. With those powerful bulldog jaws, he bit the wire in half.

It was as if Sarge knew that he had only a split second to do the deed or he, too, would be frozen by the electrical charge and become as helpless as they were.

Although he accomplished the heroic deed, he could not escape the effects of the powerful electric charge. Sarge fell dead the instant his jaws snapped the wire. My brother and uncle survived only because of Sarge's unselfish act of sacrifice.

Later, the doctor who examined my brother said that his heart could not have handled very much more of the electrical current.

I have always wondered just how it was that old Sarge could have understood that my brother and uncle were being killed by the wire.

And even perceiving that, how did he know that the wire must be cut in order to save their lives?

Benjamin Smith

Eight months after my husband died, I accepted my cousin's invitation to take a job with his business in another city. Kent had always been a good friend, as well as family, and he argued that I should start over in a new environment that wouldn't be loaded with so many memories. He and his wife Eve would be happy to help us get settled.

My husband Joel had been a history teacher and the head football coach at the high school in the small Idaho community where we had lived for nearly ten years. At all the away games, Joel and the girls' physical ed teacher would drive a van with the cheerleaders while his assistant coach rode on the bus with the team.

On a foggy October night, the van had been struck at a railroad crossing by a fast-moving freight train. Joel, the physical ed teacher, and all but one of the five cheerleaders were killed outright. The girl survived, but would be confined to a wheelchair for the rest of her life.

After the funeral and a brief mourning period, a number of the parents began preparations to sue the high school, claiming that Joel, who had been driving, had been at fault in the accident. Ugly rumors began to fly around the small town, even some suggesting that Joel, a firm, lifelong teetotaler, had been drinking.

Kent was right. It was becoming extremely unpleasant living in the beautiful village that we had loved so very much. Thankfully, he remembered my secretarial skills—and he claimed that he really needed a secretary now that his loyal gal Friday was retiring at the age of seventy-six. The timing was just right to relocate to the medium-sized city in Washington State where Kent had his factory. We moved in early August so that my sons, Shawn, eight, and Scott, six, could be settled before school started.

We had barely gotten moved into the small but attractive house that I had bought with the insurance money when the boys came home one day followed by a scruffy, mangy-looking cur. "Please, please, can we keep him?"

They had already named him Max, and there was no question that in spite of his woebegone, unkempt appearance, the mutt had a winning way about him.

And there was no question but that he was a stray, probably dumped on the streets by some irresponsible jerk who had grown tried of keeping him. He wore no collar, and he was skin and bones from lack of proper nourishment. I'm no expert, but I guessed that with his medium-length, yellowish hair, he was some kind of Labrador-setter mix.

If we were to keep him, I told the boys, we would have to have a veterinarian check him out. Shawn and Scott cheered in unison, interpreting my warning as consent.

The vet, a seemingly cheery man in all other respects, was not at all positive about our keeping Max. After a rather extensive examination, he guess-timated Max's age at around two years; then he rattled off at least half a dozen ailments that he suspected Max harbored, and he listed several more shots and pills that Max should have immediately. In answer to my legitimate query as to how much this would cost me, he shrugged and rounded off a fee at around seven hundred dollars.

My knees buckled. After the move, the purchase of the house, and buying some new clothes suitable for work, I was nearly broke. Seven hundred dollars would just about clean out the cupboard until my first paycheck.

"Mrs. S., my advice, if you want it," he began — then taking notice of Shawn and Scott for the first time, dropping his voice to a whisper — "is to let me put the dog to sleep. I don't think he's worth saving. And he's certainly not worth that much money."

He had not lowered his voice nearly enough. Shawn understood the euphemism of putting a dog "to sleep," and he quickly translated for Scott. Tears brimmed in their eyes.

"No, please, Momma," Scott pleaded. "Let him live, please."

My sons had had too much of death in their young lives. I told the vet to begin patching up our dog so we could take him home with us as soon as possible.

Even Kent was critical of my decision, arguing that if I wanted to get the boys a dog, he had a friend who would sell us a purebred at a very reasonable price, less than I would be paying in veterinarian's bills for a mutt of absolutely no pedigree whatsoever. I asked him to be understanding. As far as Shawn and Scott were concerned, it had to be Max.

By Christmastime, we had had Max for four months. He had regained his health—and his appetite. He had filled out into quite a handsome canine, and he seemed to bring some kind of balance to Shawn and Scott that had made their adjustment to new schools and a new community much easier.

Because of the meaning that he brought to my sons' lives, I overlooked the bills that demonstrated that he was nearly eating us out of house and home. And he wasn't satisfied with crummy old dog food and scraps. He had developed a sweet tooth and would sit up and beg for chocolate chip cookies.

Even worse than his bottomless tummy was the fact that Max seemed never to stop shedding hair. His yellowish strands would stick to the sofa, drift across the carpet, end up in the laundry, and even float up to our plates at mealtime.

But in spite of all these minor irritations, I had to admit that I loved Max as much as the boys did.

Three nights before Christmas, Max awakened me by pawing at my covers and whining. I had been working overtime at the office to get extra holiday money, and I did not appreciate his intrusion into my room.

"Just let me sleep and get out of here, you bad dog!" I scolded him. "You know my bedroom is off limits when I'm sleeping! Bad dog!"

His response was a sharp bark that hurt my eardrums.

And then I sat up, wide awake. Max always slept between the boys. In four months he had never entered my bedroom at night.

Something was wrong.

Then I noticed that the power on my alarm clock wasn't working.

Figuring that we had experienced a power outage, I slid my feet over the side of the bed and into my slippers. I had foolishly left on too many Christmas lights and had blown a fuse, no doubt. Max had probably become upset by the sudden darkness in the house.

As I stumbled around my bedroom in the dark, Max kept barking that shrill, ear-piercing yelp.

Would he be that upset by the darkness? Or was something else wrong in the house?

When I opened the hall closet where the circuit breakers were located, I nearly fell to my knees in horror. There was a huge wall of flame and smoke inside. And my opening the door had caused smoke to billow out in dark, suffocating clouds. I began to choke in uncontrollable spasms as I staggered backwards.

Animal Miracles ～ 67

The fire had obviously burned out the circuit breakers so the smoke detectors couldn't go off. The flames and the smoke had been traveling up the inside wall of the hallway, eating away at the house's very structure.

I was trembling in terror. Would I even be able to get to the boys' room before the walls and ceilings were engulfed in flames? The smoke moved around me in smothering clouds that made me choke and gasp and blinded my vision.

Just as I was about to panic, Max took my wrist in his mouth and led me through the smoke to the door to my sons' room.

I hesitated, afraid to open the door. What if their room, too, was filled with flames? What if Shawn and Scott were already burned alive?

I thought I would collapse with fear. If the boys were dead, there was no reason for me to live. I would just lie down and give up and let the flames take me.

Max shook my wrist, as if prompting me to stay focused, to stay centered. I opened the door and saw to my relief and joy that it had only just begun to fill with smoke.

Once inside the room, Max barked sharply, then bounded to the double bed to nudge Shawn and Scott into wakefulness. Although they were understandably dazed and confused, Max shepherded them toward me, then led us all through the thick smoke to safety out the front door.

Although the fire department arrived within minutes, our house sustained heavy damage, forcing us to accept lodging with Kent and Eve until we could find a new home.

"Max saved our lives, didn't he, Momma?" Scott asked as I was tucking him and Shawn into bed in their guest room.

When Shawn and I readily agreed that Max was a hero, Scott corrected us by saying that he was an angel.

"After Daddy died," he told us, "I prayed that God would send an angel to watch over us. I knew he heard me when he sent Max to protect us. Now Max even worked a miracle and saved us from a burning house. He is a real angel for sure."

Charlene S.

*J**ust* to prove that no creature is too small or insignificant to be capable of saving your life under the right circumstances, the late Ian Currie, a former University of Toronto lecturer, shared this amazing story of a rat rescue:

There was an elderly man in West Virginia who was a coal miner. He owned the mine he worked in, but he often noticed that he was sharing the dark tunnel with another creature—a rat. This was a unique rat that would always seem to stay near him as he worked. It was as if the rat was keeping him company—and vice versa.

Over a period of several months, the two became quite content with each other. They had established some patterns that worked well, and one might even say they had a kind of "bonding" with each other.

When the miner would sit down to eat from his lunch box, he would always feed the rat some scraps from his own meal. When it came time to fire the shots that would bring down a coal face, the miner made sure that he chased the rat away so it would not be injured in the blast.

One day, while the miner was working alone in the mine, the rat appeared to be unduly agitated. It scurried back and forth, scampering up to the miner, then running off. It repeated this behavior so often that the miner began to get the feeling that the little rat was trying to tell him something.

Intrigued as to what in the world this was about, the miner put down his drill and followed the rat around the corner to see if he could figure out what was bothering the little creature. The miner had just barely moved away from the mining face of the coal mine when the roof collapsed. The cave-in of the roof had occurred *exactly* in the spot the miner had been standing in!

Currie said that the miner would surely have been killed without the warning of his friend the rat. "But how the rat knew the roof was about to collapse, and why he warned the man, is presently one of the mysteries of animal–human interaction, I think," Currie said. He then added that "the rat employed an animal's intuition for danger, and somehow it was able to communicate with the human who had befriended it."

I was in Jasper, in Alberta, Canada, one summer a couple of years ago. The resort where I was staying was on a lake near Pyramid Mountain—rugged, gorgeous country.

One day I had walked along the road with a friend to a beautiful spot where there was a magnificent view of a small island in the lake. My friend wanted to sit awhile near the lake, and I decided to take the woods trail back to the cabin.

I cut through brush and trees to get up to the path, and on the way I had a fearful thought: What if a wild and fierce animal were up there somewhere? What would I do if I suddenly encountered some ferocious creature?

I pushed the fear aside and kept walking up to the trail.

When I got there, I saw that I was sharing the path with a large female deer or elk. Although I am not an experienced appraiser of wildlife, the animal was so large that it was most likely an elk. When she saw me emerge from the brush, she began to walk toward me. I backed up, frightened, wondering if she was going to charge me.

Then she slowly turned around and began walking the same trail that I had to follow to get back to my cabin.

For a few agonizing moments, I was puzzled as to what to do, for there was no other trail of which I was aware that would take me back to where I needed to go. There was no question: I had to walk that same trail in the same direction as the very large undomesticated creature walking ahead of me.

I had no choice. There was nothing for me to do but to follow the elk.

The elk stayed on the trail until she approached a smaller path that I would have to follow to reach my cabin. To my astonishment, she left the larger trail at exactly that point and began to walk the smaller path that I must take. Once again, I followed the large female elk as she trod the path until it met the grassy area near my cabin.

I could only shake my head in wonder. The large female elk that I had at first feared had walked me back home, right up to my cabin door.

I watched her move gracefully, elegantly behind the cabin—and then she disappeared.

Try as I might, I couldn't spot the big female elk anywhere back on the path, the larger trail—or anywhere within eyesight in the woods near my cabin. She had just disappeared.

As I considered all that had transpired, it occurred to me that Spirit had just given me a big lesson in trusting and in removing fear from our lives. I had been reminded that we are all protected in God's love and light.

Shirley Hessel

*T*hree sisters had been missing for nearly fourteen hours in the frozen woodlands of upper Minnesota. It was a miserable late winter's day in 1994, and somewhere Danielle, twelve, Delia, ten, and Dory, eight, were cold, hungry, and very lost.

Perhaps every single one of the nearly five hundred volunteers and law enforcement officers heard a similar monologue repeating itself over and over inside his or her head while they desperately searched for the Stevenson sisters:

How long can they last in the chilling cold and the heavy rain? . . . My God, how would I feel if those were my kids out there in those dark and cold woods?

The girls' father, forty-year-old Walter, who had joined the search party, said that his three daughters, their dog Jack, and their friend, thirteen-year-old Emily Colwell, had been out exploring in the woods, pretending to be pioneer women. As Emily and Jack, who were in the lead, crossed a pond, the ice cracked behind them, preventing the Stevenson sisters from following.

"What will we do now?" Emily asked. "We're separated!"

"Do you think you can find your way back to our place from here?" Danielle asked their friend.

Emily looked about her, carefully studying the area. "I'm pretty sure that I can. I think I was here once before with my dad. It looks kind of familiar to me."

"So you think you'll be all right?" Danielle wanted to be certain. "I mean, about finding your way back to our house?"

"Pretty sure," Emily nodded. "And I'll have Jack with me. He should be able to find your house. What about you? Will you be all right?"

"Don't worry about us," Delia told her. "We'll get home another way. I know a shortcut."

"I want to go with Emily and Jack," little Dory protested. "I don't want to go on Delia's shortcut."

"I'm sure you don't, Dory," Danielle sighed, rolling her eyes impatiently. "But do you want to jump in the icy water and swim across to them?"

Dory shook her head emphatically. "No way! I would freeze to death!"

"Genius girl!" Danielle grinned broadly, patting her little sister on the head in mock approval. "Good thinking. So I guess that's why you'll stay with us."

Emily reappraised their situation. "Are you sure you know your way back? Maybe you should wait right there until Jack and I come back with help."

"No problem, Em," Delia said confidently. "Like I said, I know a really good shortcut. I'll bet you that we'll beat you home!"

Emily smiled and said that she would take that bet. She waved goodbye to her friends; then she and the Stevensons' dog, Jack, a sturdy beagle, set off on the path on the other side of the pond.

Emily and Jack made it back to the Stevensons' with no difficulty.

But in spite of Delia's confident assertion about a shortcut, Danielle, Delia, and Dory did not come home.

That first night, forty volunteers with flashlights searched the dark, frozen woodlands in heavy rain. The searchers were acutely aware that the young girls had no blankets or camping gear with them. It was unlikely that they even had a match with them to light a fire. In spite of their heavy winter clothing, they would be chilled to the bone.

And then the rain turned to snow and the forest became even more treacherous.

At home, Bonnie Stevenson prayed for the safety of her daughters. A woman of great faith and spiritual strength, she knew that Danielle, Delia, and Dory needed a miracle—and she was praying unceasingly that one would be granted.

At the same time, cold reality kept intruding on her thoughts, reminding her that the girls' chances for survival were very slim.

Jack seemed puzzled by all the confusion and distress around him. He began to pace back and forth in the Stevenson kitchen, whining, whimpering, obviously very upset.

When he could not stand to wait or to pace nervously one minute longer, Jack slipped unnoticed out of the Stevenson house and went in search of the three girls.

By morning the search party of humans had grown from forty to nearly five hundred.

But Jack didn't need a small army to help him find Danielle, Delia, and Dory. In fact, he found them quite easily all by himself.

"It's good old Jack come to save us," Delia said when the beagle came upon their makeshift camp between two fallen trees. The girls had managed to pile branches over the trunks and fashion a crude kind of shelter against the rain and snow.

The sisters began to cry and laugh at the same time. Just the very sight of Jack raised their spirits, and they hugged him lovingly as he went from one to the other, licking their faces.

"If Jack can find us," Danielle reasoned, "Dad and Mom and anyone else who's looking for us should surely be able to find us."

Dory put her arms around the beagle's powerful shoulders. "Please show us the way home, Jack. I want to go home right now!"

Danielle shook her head. "No, we're staying put. We walked enough yesterday."

"And all we did was walk around in circles," Delia added wearily.

"Taking your wonderful shortcut, smarty-pants!" Dory scowled.

"Enough," Danielle said. "Look at Jack. See the way he's curled up beside us? That's a sign that he wants us to stay here. We'll all just huddle and cuddle close around him and pool our body heat. That's how we'll stay warm until someone finds us."

Jack stayed with the girls until they were found— nearly twenty-two hours after they had been reported missing.

Bonnie Stevenson was granted her miracle, and her daughters were assessed as being in pretty good condition considering the ordeal that they had been through in the freezing rain, snow, and cold.

Jack was given a big steak as a reward for finding Danielle, Delia, and Dory when nearly five hundred humans could not.

*O*n June 2, 1974, Mrs.
Cassandra Villanueva,
fifty-two, was on board the *Aloha* when it caught fire and
sank six hundred miles south of Manila, in the
Philippines. Unable to make it to a lifeboat, the woman
grabbed a life jacket and was tossed to the fickle mercy
of the ocean.

Forty-eight hours later, Mrs. Villanueva was spotted
by the *Kalantia*, a Philippine naval vessel. The sailors
who made the initial sighting stated that the woman
appeared to be clinging to an oil drum.

However, as the vessel drew nearer the fortunate
survivor and someone threw her a life preserver, the
sailors involved in the rescue said that the oil drum
suddenly sank from view. It was only when the team was
hauling Mrs. Villanueva up to the deck of the *Kalantia*
that they saw that she had been clutching the shell of a
giant sea turtle.

According to reports in several international wire
services, one of her rescuers stated that the giant turtle
was first sighted beneath Mrs. Villanueva, propping her
up. It even circled the area twice before disappearing
into the depths of the sea, as if to reassure itself that its
former passenger was in good hands.

Mrs. Villanueva told reporters that after the *Aloha*
sank, she had been floating in the water for more than

twelve hours when the giant sea turtle appeared beneath her and lifted her out of the water. She said that its head was as large as that of a big dog.

Later, a very small turtle climbed on Mrs. Villanueva's back as she rode on the giant turtle's shell.

As if the small turtle had appointed itself her assistant guardian against the dangers of the sea, she said that it bit her every time she felt drowsy. She mused that it was as if it wished to prevent her from submerging her head beneath the waves and drowning.

It seemed especially appropriate to Naiomi Johnston that she would give birth to her daughter on Valentine's Day, February 14, 1993. And while she was recuperating in the hospital, her husband Darryl and their three-year-old son Donald were at home in Midland, Ontario, surrounded by snowdrifts, eagerly anticipating the return of mother and brand-new baby sister.

Little Donald was eager to see his mommy and his baby sister. He really missed Mommy, and he just couldn't wait to see what a sister would look like.

Daddy told him that he had to wait awhile. It was very cold outside, and there were snowdrifts as high as mountains. Travel, he had said sternly, was out of the question.

But Donald couldn't imagine that those snowbanks could stop his little electric toy car. He could see no reason why he couldn't just get into his own little car and drive off to the hospital and visit Mommy and sister. If Daddy didn't want to go, well, he could just wait at home.

Just in case Daddy might object to his setting out to visit Mommy and baby sister, Donald got up really early, while Daddy was still sleeping, and set out in his electric car to drive to the hospital.

It didn't take long for the car's battery to run down, and pretty soon it wouldn't move at all.

Not to worry. It couldn't be that far to the hospital. He would walk the rest of the way.

Once he started walking, it didn't take Donald very long to realize that Daddy was right. It really was very, very cold. And the snowdrifts were as high as mountains.

And he was lost. He had no idea where he was.

Constable Kirk Wood of the Ontario Provincial Police told journalist Esmond Choueke that at this point little Donald Johnston was probably less than thirty minutes from death. The three-year-old boy had no real protection from the cold, blowing wind.

But Donald apparently had two guardian angels on duty that cold morning in Ontario—one from heaven and another from a nearby farm.

Brian Holmes was outside his farmhouse doing chores with Samantha, his six-year-old German shepherd, when he noticed that the big dog was acting strangely, as if she sensed something was wrong. All of a sudden, she lifted her head, sniffed the air, and ran toward the woods.

Although Samantha's actions were somewhat peculiar, Holmes finally concluded that she had picked up the scent of a rabbit or some other animal, and he went on with his morning chores.

If Samantha had been able to explain her motives to her master, she might have informed him that she had far more serious concerns on that frigid morning than chasing rabbits through the snow. A sense beyond her physical sensory abilities had told her that somewhere a small human child was in a desperate situation.

Samantha found the three-year-old sitting under a tree, cold and crying. She licked his face and nudged him to his feet. She knew that the little human must not rest in any one place for very long or he would freeze to death. She kept him on his feet and continued to push him in the direction of the farmhouse.

To Donald's eyes, Samantha must have seemed like a big, furry angel. He threw his arms around her neck and allowed her to guide him along whatever path she felt was best. To his three-year-old mind, the trees bending and moaning in the cold wind and the eight-foot-high snowdrifts must have seemed like a frozen nightmare. But somehow he knew that this big dog would bring him back to warmth and life.

Brian Holmes had just begun to wonder about his German shepherd when he spotted her coming down the road with a small boy hanging on to her for dear life. He immediately brought Donald inside the farmhouse, fed him, and let him get nice and warm.

The farmer gave his dog an affectionate scratch behind her ear. Somehow, in a mysterious way beyond his ability to ascertain, Samantha had been able to sense that there was a little lost boy somewhere out there among the snowdrifts and the freezing cold. She had found Donald, and in that marvelous expression of symbiotic relationship between humans and canines, she brought him to their home so her master could keep him warm and preserve his spark of life.

*M*y wife and I were enjoying a sunset walk on a beach in Washington State when we came upon an interesting group composed of a very upset young woman, her horse, a person who was apparently her friend, and another individual who was quite obviously a stranger to all the others. Since upset young women and horses are not commonly encountered on ocean beaches, my attention became riveted upon the little drama playing out before us.

My wife and I learned that the young woman and her friend had completed an enjoyable day of riding— and then a tragic event had occurred. She had lost a precious possession on the beach, a gold watch that had been given to her by her father, who had only recently passed on.

Then, as we understood it, the couple had prevailed upon a man who was a stranger to them to hold the horse and stay on the beach while they sought the assistance of others in the nearby town to return with them to search for the missing precious possession. It was immediately apparent that they had been unable to gain any additional searchers and they had returned to the beach alone to try once again to find the lost watch.

They must have been desperate to have asked the particular stranger who presently held the reins of the horse. He had obviously been beach-partying all day, and I could see that the horse sensed his abandoned and carefree nature.

He and the horse circled each other in the sand, the stranger with a beer in one hand and the horse's reins in the other. The horse eyed him warily, uncomfortably stomping a compacted circle twenty feet across and making occasional snorts of discomfort.

Judging by the extent and the depth of the compacted sand, the horse and the stranger had been engaged in this face-off for quite some time.

As we drew nearer the distraught woman and her friend, I overheard her say that they were about to leave on another mission to get help in their quest to locate the lost watch. What they thought this would gain was uncertain. Reason and logic had long since departed.

As I looked at the young woman, I sensed a plea for help, somehow echoed by a glance at the horse.

Through her tears, she told me of her deep spiritual connection with her father's gold watch. As I learned more about the situation, I felt sympathy for her in her sense of loss — and I also grew increasingly concerned that the horse might break in fear and perhaps injure someone.

I touched the horse to calm him. I have kept horses for a long time, and I fully acknowledge the love and understanding shown us by the species. Maybe the cowboy hat I was wearing helped, for the horse also acknowledged my love and respect for his species.

After touching the young woman's wrist, I stepped into the well-compacted circle and stood briefly, sensing.

I took two or three steps around the circle.

I still don't know whether it was psychic intervention or animal communication that led me to dip my big toe into the sand.

But I do know that *without the horse, this would not have been*.

I lifted the missing gold watch from the sand atop my big toe. The sight of the chain link glinting in the rays of the setting sun was as shocking to me as it was to its relieved young owner.

There had been no searching, no digging, no doubt—just pure communication.

We all stood frozen for precious moments, realizing that something rather special had occurred.

The stranger, relieved of his awesome responsibility, passed me the reins of the horse and began silently walking away down the beach.

The rest of us spent a few moments in trivial conversation, but the shining moment transcended all. We had experienced something real.

Kevin

In August of 1996, a number of newspapers in Great Britain carried the remarkable story of how a farmer's fair treatment of his cattle came full circle when the bovine ladies worked together to save him from death at the hooves of an enraged bull.

Fifty-four-year-old Donald Mottram had driven his four-wheel bike into a field on his farm in Meidrim, near Carmarthen, Wales, to give a calf an injection.

Before he gave himself totally to the task, Mottram checked the location of a three-year-old French Charolais bull that he had on loan for breeding his cattle—a mixture of Welsh Blacks and Aberdeen Angus—and saw that the 3,300-pound brute was at least three hundred yards away. Satisfied that the bull was quiet and uninterested in his presence, Mottram directed his attention to the injured calf that he hoped would one day become a member of the breeding herd of ninety cattle that he kept on his farm.

He was shepherding the calf when he suddenly felt a "horrendous thump" on his back. Mottram and his bike were tossed thirty feet away.

He landed on his back, and as he lay there in a daze, he found himself looking up into the snorting, enraged face of the bull.

The powerful young bull began trampling the farmer, stomping on his chest and shoulders. Mottram tried to turn away, but the huge animal kicked him into unconsciousness.

Later, he estimated that he had been unconscious for ninety minutes, and when he came to, he saw that he was surrounded by a large group of his cattle. And it was immediately apparent that Daisy, his fourteen-year-old "bell cow," had taken charge of the ladies and that they had formed a protective circle around him.

Daisy had always been one of Mottram's special favorites. Whenever he wanted the herd back in the barns, all he had to do was to call Daisy, and she would lead the other cattle back home. And now she had saved his life by marshaling the other cows to join in standing with her against the bull.

As he lay injured and dazed within the circle of cattle, Mottram could hear the bull snorting, stamping the ground, and bellowing his rage. From time to time, he would charge into the circle of cattle, but Daisy would see to it that the wall of bovine flesh held firm.

With Daisy keeping the circle of cattle intact and shielding him, Mottram was able to crawl two hundred yards to the gate and get to the house so he could call for help.

He was in the hospital for six days with a dislocated jaw, broken ribs, damaged lungs, and bruised shoulders. In addition, there was a hoofprint on his chest that took five months to heal.

When he was asked for his explanation of why he thought Daisy and the others had intervened and taken up his cause against the bull, he replied, "I have treated the animals reasonably, and they have looked after me in return. People say that I am too soft, but I believe you reap what you sow."

Eight-year-old Natasha Eberling set out on a lovely August day in 1996 on what she intended to be a pleasant nature walk with her beloved twelve-year-old collie, Belle. The Eberling family always joked that Belle was Natasha's older sister, for in the four years before their daughter had been born, the collie had been their only "child."

Girl and dog had been virtually inseparable since Natasha's birth, but this summer she had decided to spend extra time with Belle, for she had overheard her parents talking about how old the faithful collie was getting to be and how she might not be around that much longer.

Poor old Belle was blind in one eye, and she seemed to take turns limping on each of her hind legs. Natasha's father had said it had something to do with Belle's hips and that it happened to a lot of big dogs when they got older. It made Natasha cry just thinking about a time when she might not have Belle at her side.

The two companions had not walked far from their home in central Minnesota when Natasha accidentally stepped directly on a beehive.

"Oh, I'm sorry. I'm so sorry. I didn't mean to step on your home!" Natasha said as she desperately attempted to explain her mistake to the angry bees.

Unfortunately for the little girl and her dog, the indignant bees weren't buying any apology for such an outrageous act of destruction to their hive. Natasha soon understood that the buzz going around the hive meant that the bees were out for revenge.

Natasha had suffered only a couple of painful stings when Belle pushed her aside and selflessly lay her long-haired collie body over the hive, thereby smothering the majority of the bees before they could become airborne and attack. Because of Belle's quick and selfless action, Natasha endured only five bee stings.

Belle, of course, was peppered and drilled with stings wherever any outraged bee had managed to get through her thick hair, and Natasha wept along with her dear collie every time Belle yelped in painful protest as a stinger struck home.

Thankfully, it wasn't terribly long before Natasha's mother heard the ruckus and started along the path in the direction of the yelps and screams. When she came upon the startling scene, she called for her husband to bring a couple of blankets and an insect fogger.

Amazingly, after a few days at the veterinarian's, Belle was back and seemingly in better shape than before.

There is an old folk belief that there is something in a bee sting that can help someone who suffers from arthritis. Maybe all those bee stings did Belle some good.

*A*ccording to M. Jean King, president of Independence Dogs, Inc. (IDI) of Chadds Ford, Pennsylvania, every story in her files is a miracle. Jean King's IDI is a nonprofit school that provides highly trained service dogs for children and adults with mobility impairments.

"We teach these special dogs to provide all the physical, psychological, and therapeutic support their human partners need to lead full, productive, *independent* lives," she said.

Jean King herself is disabled and knows firsthand the challenge of facing everyday life with a physical impairment. A clinical microbiologist, concert organist, and amateur athlete, Jean was thirty-nine when she contracted tuberculosis of the spine (Pott's disease). After eighteen months of operations and body casts, she was informed that she would have to spend the rest of her life in a wheelchair.

For one who had been so active and so self-reliant, Jean found it extremely difficult to have to rely on others for everything from picking up her groceries at the supermarket to picking up the pen she had dropped on the floor. After several months of such dependence on others, she began to foresee that the growing loss of her sense of identity and self-respect would be a far greater deprivation than the loss of her ability to walk.

Jean began to train her dog, Shantih, to take the place of her legs and her mobility. Somehow, Jean reasoned, it should be possible to train Shantih to work with her so that they could become a team, a unit that would function as one. When she sensed Shantih's willingness to be of service and saw her intelligent responses to instruction, Jean realized that her faithful dog was striving to give her life back to her.

In 1984, after spending fourteen years working with dogs, Jean emerged as a nationally recognized authority on training service dogs—and with the full awareness that the miracle that she had accomplished with Shantih must be shared with others. Impassioned with a true sense of mission and a deep empathy for those who suffered mobility impairments, she used her own experiences with Shantih to develop Independence Dogs, a training school built around her own unique teaching philosophy and techniques.

Jean is quick to stress the point that any school that claims to train dogs for such demanding service to the mobility impaired must understand *all* the challenges faced by such individuals and must recognize both their physical and their emotional needs.

"This is what sets us apart from other service dog schools," she said. "That is why IDI is the only school recommended by the Seeing Eye and one of a handful of schools recommended by the Delta Society for our adaptability to serve exceptional cases."

Such an "exceptional case" was that of Matt, a former March of Dimes poster child, who first came to IDI when he was ten.

Matt had been born without arms and knee joints. If he fell, he was unable to get back up on his feet. If he were playing alone, Matt could fall and lie helplessly for several minutes before someone might notice and come to help him.

Because his doctors had not expected Matt to grow, he was first paired with a smaller dog, Ginger, a collie-mix. If Matt should ever fall in her presence, Ginger was trained to stand and brace him while he pressed his back against her shoulder and worked his way back up to a standing position. She also turned lights on and off, pushed elevator buttons, and carried Matt's books and supplies in her saddle bags.

For the first time in his life, Matt was able to attend school like all the other kids his age and not have to depend on anyone for help. Ginger had become his arms.

Over the next three years, Matt defied his doctors' earlier prognosis and outgrew Ginger. At that point, IDI paired him with Rocky, a golden retriever, specially selected for his size, temperament, and ability to suit Matt's needs.

"When Matt was eighteen, his mother sent us a letter with a copy of his high school graduation picture," Jean said. "She also told us that Matt and

Rocky had gone to the senior prom with Matt's date. Matt is now attending the University of Delaware with plans to become an attorney. And Rocky is still carrying Matt's books to class."

In other cases from M. Jean King's files:

Michele, who has had cerebral palsy since birth, calls Noble "a miracle dog, a true gift from God." Noble helps Michele with counter exchanges at stores, opens doors for her, presses elevator buttons, and does a score of other daily tasks that most of us take for granted.

Ten-year-old Samantha was born with spina bifida, and in her mind, her Independence Dog Tucker helps her to feel more independent. "Tucker is my best friend," Samantha said. "I feel less like a baby now. I don't need to ask people for help anymore. I love Tucker."

Irene, who has Friedrich's ataxia, a peripheral nerve disease, cannot imagine life without Snickers. He helps with household tasks such as gathering laundry, accompanies Irene on shopping excursions, braces for transfers from wheelchair to bed, and helps his partner up if she should fall. "Snix has given me back my lost freedom," she said. "People are constantly amazed at what I manage to accomplish with his help."

Steve, who contracted Parkinson's disease when he was in his late twenties, said that he used to fall ninety times a day because of his affliction. People used to stare at him, thinking he was a drunk or a drug addict. Now, with his Independence Dog Rocco at his side, Steve falls as few as eight times a day and is even able to jog with his canine companion at his side.

Two years ago Jenelle, a student at the University of Illinois, was diagnosed with dystonia, a neurological movement disorder that makes walking extremely difficult. But with Kramer to pull her wheelchair around the large campus and up steep ramps, she regularly beats her fellow students to class.

Today M. Jean King's faithful companion is Darshan, whose devotion and strength she acknowledged in a poem she composed containing the following lines:

> No, Darsh, you can't release me from my chair
> but you've made my life worth living from there.
> Your presence and help empower me to face
> any challenge, any time, any place.

Jean's compassionate and inspired training of her Independence Dogs has returned freedom and self-respect to many men, women, and children throughout the United States. And during all the years of her training school's growth and accomplishment, she has never forgotten the miracle of the beautiful soul she declares the "true founder of Independence Dogs," the loving Shantih, who passed on in 1996 at the age of thirteen.

M. Jean King, President
Independence Dogs, Inc.
Chadds Ford, PA

*O*n January 15, 1990, eighteen-year-old Lotty Stevens and a friend embarked on a fishing trip from Port Vila, Vanuatu, an island in the South Pacific. Although both young men were experienced fishermen, they were caught off guard by a sudden storm that capsized their boat.

Helplessly, Lotty and his friend were tossed about by waves as they desperately sought to stay above the water. Fortunately for Lotty, it was his habit always to slip on a life jacket when fishing in the ocean.

Later, when the sea was calmer and the waves had subsided, he looked around the wreckage of their boat for his friend. After calling his name for several minutes, Lotty was forced to conclude that his companion had drowned during the storm.

For three days, Lotty clung to the overturned boat, bobbing lazily up and down as the wreckage drifted aimlessly. Then, with only his life jacket for support, he decided to swim in the direction in which he felt Port Vila lay.

For two days, the teenager alternated swimming as hard as he could, then floating and resting, praying all the while for a miracle. If only some fishing boats would come upon him and rescue him.

He tried hard to fight against despair. He knew that even a large ship could pass relatively close by and not be able to see his head bobbing in the vast ocean.

Toward the end of the fifth day after the raging storm had sent him into the sea, Lotty Stevens got his miracle. He had been floating with his eyes closed when he felt something big lift him from the water. There beneath him was a giant stingray, at least eleven feet long—including its six-foot poisonous tail. And the massive sea beast was taking him for a ride.

At first Lotty was frightened. Stingrays were not known for performing benevolent acts.

But soon, he later told journalists, he began to think of the giant sea creature as his friend. He would pat it as if it were a dog. A big, slimy dog with a hard and strong body.

One afternoon, after several days as a grateful hitchhiker, Lotty suddenly found himself dumped in the water as the stingray dove and disappeared. Lotty shook his head to clear the sea from his eyes—then wished that he hadn't. An enormous shark was heading straight for him.

Dear Lord, he silently screamed, why had his friend left him now? Was the stingray afraid of the killer beast coming toward him?

Then the teenager saw a second shark—and a third. Suddenly Lotty's angel of the sea reappeared, swimming in a fast circle around him. Amazingly, the three sharks turned fin and swam away. Apparently they feared the stingray's long, poisonous tail more than they felt the desire to feed on a human.

Lotty gave his thanks to God and the stingray that had once again saved his life. The great sea creature came alongside Lotty and nudged him, so he climbed back on board its strong back.

Until the joyous morning when he at last sighted land, the teenager survived for eight more days by catching fish from atop his seaborne savior. The stingray also spotted the beach, for it headed for the shallow water and slid Lotty off near the shoreline.

Lotty remembered staggering like a drunken man, then collapsing on the sandy beach. The next morning he was awakened by a fisherman.

It took the teenager several moments to realize that he was not dreaming and that he was actually once again on solid land. As he slowly came to appreciate the fact that he was no longer in danger of drowning or of being eaten by sharks, he also realized with a sudden pang of regret that he hadn't had a chance to thank his remarkable friend from the ocean for saving his life.

The fisherman helped Lotty to a doctor, and later, a hospital on the main island pronounced the teenager in good shape except for some dehydration and a few sores from saltwater and chafing against his life jacket. When he telephoned his family, their grief turned to joy beyond understanding, for they had already held a funeral service for him. It had been twenty-one days since Lotty and his friend had disappeared in the ocean storm.

Lotty does not argue with those who would seek to disbelieve the facts of his remarkable rescue. He is living proof that somehow he survived twenty-one boatless days adrift in the ocean. In the opinion of Lotty Stevens and his family, that most certainly qualifies as a miracle.

It was a quiet winter's day at Chris Georgiou's trout-fishing farm outside of Adelaide, Australia. No one had arrived to cast fishing lines in the picturesque area of the lake that he had dammed for hopeful anglers, so he was taking advantage of the off-day to catch up on some maintenance chores. First on the list would be to cut down some of the tall grass that had grown up on the banks.

With his wife away on vacation in Africa and no customers in sight, Georgiou was completely alone on the farm—with the exception of Ziggy, his two-year-old border collie, and Stella, his two-year-old rottweiler.

Ziggy stayed close at his side as Georgiou chopped at the tall grass on the bank, while Stella dozed in the sun outside the house about sixty yards away.

Georgiou remembers that he stood to straighten himself in order to ease the strain on his back caused by the bending posture that he was forced to assume as he hacked away at the grass. He absentmindedly forgot how close he was to the iron railing that surrounded the fishing area, and as he rose he gave his head a solid rap on one of the iron bars.

Stunned, he staggered backward, lost his balance, and fell into the icy water of the lake. Because it was a chilly day, Georgiou was wearing a heavy wool sweater, a thick overcoat, overalls, and boots. The bulky clothing caused him to sink as if he were draped with lead weights. Such heavy, cumbersome clothing would have taxed the strength of even an accomplished swimmer, but the sixty-six-year-old trout farmer had never learned to swim a stroke.

Desperately thrashing his arms in the water and shouting for help, Georgiou knew it was only a matter of time before he drowned.

There was no one around for miles who could hear his cries for help, and his frantic and involuntary kicking and flailing movements were only propelling him even farther away from shore.

Faithful Ziggy, who never left his master's side, stood on the bank, sounding a shrill, frightened bark. It was obvious to Georgiou that the little border collie wanted to help, but he seemed to have an awareness that his compact twenty-five-pound body could do little to keep both of them afloat.

Georgiou coughed and sputtered, realizing grimly that his desperate struggle for life was nearly over. It seemed to him at that moment that the last sound he would hear on Earth would be the mournful bark of his loyal Ziggy.

It was at that same moment of resignation to a terrible fate that a miracle occurred that enabled Georgiou to tell journalist Chris Pritchard the whole dramatic story.

Stella, the husky rottweiler, hurtled through the air as if launched from a catapult, then splashed down in the lake beside him. Somehow, with what may have been his last ounce of strength, Georgiou managed to get hold of

Stella's right leg, and the powerfully built ninety-pound rottweiler began towing him slowly toward the bank.

Stella's courageous act rejuvenated Georgiou and gave him the resolve to hold on long enough to reach the shallows of the lake, where he might regain his footing.

Exhausted from his ordeal, he held on to the determined rottweiler until he was at last able to stand upright in the water.

Freezing cold, chilled to the bone, he managed to drag himself up the wooden steps leading out of the dammed area, and finally collapsed out of harm's way.

As he propped himself up on his elbows, the two dogs began joyously licking at his face.

Georgiou struggled to a sitting position and reached out to hug his two dogs. He later freely admitted that he cried like a baby.

After he had made his way to the house and gotten out of his wet clothing and warmed himself, Georgiou realized clearly how little Ziggy had possessed the wisdom to understand that as much as he wanted to jump into the lake to save his master, he was just too small to rescue a big man weighted down by heavy clothing. That was why he had barked so shrilly. He knew that his only chance to save Georgiou lay in his being able to rouse the snoozing Stella, who was strong as a bull, to come quickly and pull their master from the lake.

Cerise Summers will always remember the afternoon in August of 1996 when she almost prevented their seven-year-old beagle, Bambi, from chasing away a child molester who threatened her son and the daughter of a friend.

Three-year-old Troy Summers and his playmate, two-and-a-half-year-old Mika Paloma, were making little roadways in the sandbox in the Summers's fenced-in yard in a suburb of Lincoln, Nebraska. Cerise could tell from the contented sounds of their giggles that they were having a good time.

"I had Bambi inside with me," Cerise said, "because she just got too enthusiastic in her playfulness for little Mika. The energetic beagle would accidently knock her over and frighten her, then make matters worse by licking her in the face to apologize.

"Mika's mom, Anita, had just gotten a new job, and I was helping out by watching Mika until she could get a regular baby-sitter," Cerise explained.

Cerise had taught elementary school for ten years until Troy was born. "Mika and Troy got along really well, so there was no problem with letting the two of them play together. And, of course, I was used to looking after kids," she said.

Cerise moved aside the curtain on the back door window and appraised the scene. Troy was moving one of his toy trucks up the little mountain of sand that the two children had fashioned. Mika seemed contented at the moment to supervise, but she had a toy convertible in her hand, waiting to try the road they had just finished constructing in the sandbox.

"I saw no reason why I couldn't take a break from my motherly duties and watch my favorite soap opera," Cerise said. "I had never been able to see any of the afternoon soaps when I was a student or a teacher. It's amazing how quickly you can get hooked on the things."

A glass of iced tea on the coffee table at her side, her feet raised comfortably on a footstool, Cerise clicked the remote and settled back to escape for half an hour into the extraordinary problems, dilemmas, and challenges of the beautiful and handsome television characters.

"At a crucial part of the program, Bambi started whining and barking to be let out," Cerise said. "I told her to wait. To be quiet. I wasn't going to let her go out unless I was with her. I didn't want her to give poor little Mika a dog phobia for life. And I didn't want to miss the scene coming up after the commercial."

Bambi would not be quieted or put off. Normally a very obedient dog, the beagle began pacing back and forth in the room, deliberately attempting to block Cerise's view of the television set, ceaselessly whining and barking.

"Quiet!" Cerise shouted, leaning forward to smack Bambi on her butt.

Bambi nimbly avoided being struck, then snapped at Cerise.

"My mouth dropped open," Cerise remembered. "I honestly couldn't believe it. Bambi had never bitten or snapped at any of us. I was shocked.

"And maybe that brainy beagle knew that was what it would take to make me pay attention to her. Anyway, that was when I began to think seriously that something must be wrong to make her act in such a manner."

Cerise got quickly to her feet and opened the back door to let Bambi out.

"The moment she was free of the house, she began snarling and growling like she was ready to do battle with a bear," Cerise said. "I ran after her to see what had so upset her—and then I truly got the shock of my life!"

Cerise was horrified to see a strange man in their backyard. And what was worse, he had Troy under one arm and Mika under another.

"I looked around for a rake or shovel or something to attack the man and make him drop our babies," Cerise said, "but Bambi was already on him. The man drew back his leg, intending to dropkick Bambi, but she sidestepped the blow and jumped up to bite him hard in his thigh. He screamed in pain and dropped the children."

The molester made a threatening move toward Cerise, but as he turned his attention away from the dog, Bambi regained it by biting him on the ankle.

"He was cursing Bambi a blue streak, but by this time I had a garden hoe in my hands and was charging toward him," Cerise said.

"He took one look at the rage in my eyes, the hoe in my hands, and the fury in Bambi's snapping teeth, and jumped over the fence.

"That's when I really started to scream, and several neighbors came out to see what was happening.

"The perverted creep, the monster who preyed on little children, ran to a pickup parked down the street and got away. Although he had obscured the license plates on his vehicle, a number of the neighbors and I were able to give the police a good description of the man."

Cerise said that she gets a terrible shudder all through her body every time she thinks what might have happened to Troy and Mika if she had not finally yielded to Bambi's demands to be let out.

As a reward for her alertness and her valor, Bambi received an extra-large plate of her favorite meal—hamburger and french fries with catsup—and a promise from Cerise that she would never again ignore her promptings to go outside.

"*Meow!* Meow!" I heard those characteristic feline sounds one day a few years ago as my mother and I were getting into our Buick Regal parked on the street in front of our apartment building in a suburb of Los Angeles. We looked all around the car, but saw no signs of a cat. Then a tiny paw suddenly emerged from beneath the car. We saw that it belonged to a scrawny, orange-striped tabby kitten, only about six months old.

My mother and I looked at each other in silent recognition of "Oh, there's the meow's owner"—when instantaneously, the kitten hopped up on her lap and proceeded to give her two kitten kisses.

Then, almost as if it wanted to be certain that I wouldn't feel left out, the kitten hopped over to me and showered me with affection of the "licking" kind.

It was then I noticed that the poor cat's tail was crooked. It looked as though it was permanently bent, possibly because of a congenital deformity or perhaps from an accident of some kind. Because of this, I named the cat Crooktail.

Mom and I supposed that the cat must be homeless, and I couldn't help but think how hard life must be for this little one. Because of his deformity, maybe he would never find a home or someone to love him. Yet he didn't seem to be aware of his abnormality or let it prevent him from pouring out unconditional love to both of us. Before Crooktail hopped out of the car, he had charmed and completely endeared himself to us.

I later discovered that Crooktail actually did have a home and owners who loved him. He had just moved into the neighborhood with his family and was just making the rounds and getting acquainted! Crooktail and I became fast friends, and actually, he made lots of friends. He quickly seemed to be the kitty friend of all the youngsters and oldsters on the entire block.

On a beautiful morning, several weeks after making Crooktail's acquaintance, as I was getting into the car, Crooktail surprised me by jumping up on my shoulder just as I was getting situated behind the wheel. I really didn't have much time for him because I was in a rush to get to an important meeting for my television show, *Beyond the Other Dominion.*

Normally, several tickles on his head and a few petting strokes would be enough to assure him that we were still friends, and he would jump out of the car and be on his merry way. But for some reason, this morning, of all mornings, when I was in such a rush, Crooktail just would not leave.

I was astonished that as I attempted to brush him ever so gently, nudging him toward the car door to "exit stage left," he simply would not budge. In fact, the more I tried to nudge him out, the more he clung to my suit jacket with his claws. The more I tried, the harder he would cling. If you have ever had a cat's claws in your clothing, you know how difficult it is to disengage them!

By now I was beginning to get a bit perturbed. Then I noticed that an old pickup truck had appeared virtually out of nowhere and was barreling down the road. It didn't take more than a split second to notice that the truck had no brakes and the driver was fighting for control of the unrestrained vehicle. As I watched, he finally brought the broken-down relic to a screeching halt at the end of the block. It was *then* that Crooktail released his grip on me and hopped out of the car voluntarily.

I sat there for a moment in a stupor. If Crooktail had not detained me by digging his claws into me, I would have been pulling out right in front of the runaway truck. Most likely, the injuries I would have sustained would have been serious, if not fatal. Although I cannot *prove* it scientifically, with the absolute certainty that I am accustomed to, I think this loving little stray kitten may have known that my life was in danger and acted to save me!

Dr. Franklin R. Ruehl, host of
Beyond the Other Dominion

Thunder, a German shepherd police dog, was inducted into the Wisconsin Pet Hall of Fame in 1996 for the heroic act of pulling Sheriff's Deputy Stanley Wontor out of an icy river.

Deputy Wontor and Thunder, his faithful K-9 partner of seven years, had been pursuing a burglary suspect across a twenty-foot-wide stretch of frozen river when the lawman crashed through the ice four feet from the snow-covered bank.

Wontor could feel the river's current pulling him under the ice-covered surface. He was certain that it would be the end of him.

He realized that his only lifeline to survival was Thunder's leash. He had wrapped the leash around his wrist when they ran in pursuit of the burglary suspect, and he still gripped it in his hand.

Fortunately the dog was powerful enough to stand his ground at the edge of the hole in the ice, and he had planted his paws solidly against the sudden pressure on his collar, thereby providing an anchor for Wontor against the current.

Although he knew that he was about to shout a command that the big German shepherd had never before heard, the deputy knew it was their only chance. He knew very well that Thunder could not withstand the pull on his leash and collar for too much longer. If the two of them did not act soon, it would be too late for both of them.

"Pull, buddy! Pull!" he yelled.

The command may have been a new one, but Thunder certainly understood that his partner did not belong in the freezing cold water of the ice-covered river.

The big German shepherd dug his powerful paws deep into the snow and began to inch backward up the bank, slowly dragging Deputy Wontor toward the edge of the hole in the ice.

Summoning hidden reserves of strength, Wontor managed to climb out of what had seemed for several terrible minutes to have been destined to become his icy coffin.

While it is certain that the fifty-five-year-old law enforcement officer, the father of three grown children, thought about his family and gave thanks for his rescue, he also remembered being "mad as a hornet." Although he was soaked to the skin and freezing, he told Thunder that the burglary suspect was not going to get away from them. Especially after he had nearly lost his life in pursuit of the man.

Amazingly, ten minutes later, Deputy Wontor and Thunder had the suspect under arrest. Later, the man led police officers to a cache of over $40,000 worth of stolen snowmobile parts, and he was subsequently convicted of burglarizing a Marinette, Wisconsin, sports center.

Reflecting on his narrow escape from the icy river, Deputy Wontor told journalist James McCandlish that as long as he lived, he would know that he owed his life to Thunder, his faithful partner and wonder dog.

I *can* truly say that I love and respect all breeds of dogs, and while I really do not wish to provoke an argument, I believe that the smaller breeds are more appropriate for apartment dwellers who live in large cities. For years now I have seen men and women walking huge canine behemoths that they can barely restrain on their leashes.

That being said, and my prejudices out in the open, I wish to tell you about something that happened to my terrier Toby and me in November of 1992.

We were doing a little neighborhood shopping in the city where I live, and I had left Toby tied up outside a grocery store while I picked up a few items for dinner.

As I entered the store, I noticed an elderly woman sitting on a bench at the bus stop. I didn't really think she was waiting for a bus, but just resting from a walk, because she was petting a cat that she had on a little leash and collar.

As I left the store with my grocery items only a few minutes later, I saw a slender, blonde girl of about fourteen or fifteen, struggling with a massive rottweiler. I sensed trouble approaching on four huge paws.

I untied Toby's leash preparatory to our walk back to the apartment, but instead of moving on, we both stood quietly observing the approach of the girl and her dog, as if we had mutually received a powerful premonition of what was about to transpire.

And then it happened. Perhaps even more horribly than we could have envisioned it.

The elderly woman set her cat down on the street and bent over to hand it some tidbit to eat. From my vantage point, I could see the rottweiler's ears prick up, and I could tell that he was a sworn member of that detestable canine society sworn to mangle and maim all felines.

I shouted twice to the woman to pick up her cat and hold it—and then I realized that she must be hard of hearing or deaf.

The cat arched its back and hissed as the rottweiler and his teenage owner came parallel to the bench. The huge brute made a lunge for the cat and jerked the young woman off balance.

"Hold on to that leash!" I shouted at the girl.

I could see that the rottweiler wore a chain choke collar that could subdue him if enough pressure were applied. It was also all too apparent that the young woman in charge of the huge dog did not have the strength or the presence of mind to apply what muscle she might have to the collar.

Her eyes were wide with panic. "I . . . I can't hold him! Magnus, stay! Stay!"

And then the rottweiler jerked loose from the girl's clutching hands, and he was free. The cat was his first victim.

Although the valiant feline got in a couple of good swipes with its claws across the monster's nose, the enraged dog took little notice of any pain inflicted as it mauled the cat mercilessly in its huge jaws and spat its bloody, crumpled body out onto the street.

The elderly woman screamed and began flailing. The rottweiler then turned and attacked her, sinking its massive jaws first into her leg, then her hand and arm, and appeared about to lunge for her throat.

It was at that moment that Toby yanked himself free of my grasp and charged the fiendish giant, his own leash trailing behind him like a knight's battle ribbon.

Unbelievably, the little terrier's surprise attack caught the rottweiler off guard, and he began to cower before Toby's onslaught. And Toby knew enough to press his advantage; he kept biting at the much larger dog's inner legs and underbelly.

I feared for my brave little Toby's life, expecting the monstrous rottweiler at any moment to realize the great disparity in their sizes and wolf Toby down in a couple of gulps. But the big dog turned out to be like so many bullies. Once he had been thrown off his vicious pace of bloody destruction, he displayed his cowardly streak and began to back away from Toby's ceaseless lunges and snapping teeth.

The teenage girl and I both reached for the rottweiler's leash, and the brute turned on his owner and bit her savagely on the thigh.

Toby, however, used the distraction to sink his teeth into the monster's private parts. The rottweiler howled in pain, and I was able to grab the leash and yank the collar around his neck hard enough to make him choke and gasp.

Thankfully, by that time a patrol car had taken notice of the melee on the street and arrived to shoot the rottweiler with a tranquilizer dart. Fortunately for us, in our city police are often forced to assume double duty as dog catchers.

An ambulance was summoned and arrived in very short order. The elderly woman was bleeding quite profusely from several wounds, and blood was soaking the teenager's jeans. It was obvious that the woman's poor cat had died instantly between the powerful jaws of the massive dog.

Toby, my own little Braveheart, had not a single wound that I could discern. All the bystanders who had observed the brief but brutal encounter from the grocery store window or from nearby apartments hailed Toby as the hero of the day. Of course, he has always been *my* hero.

Duncan W.

*S*eventeen-year-old Tawnya Sutherland of Kearns, Utah, came home on the afternoon of February 6, 1994, to find herself confronted by every young girl's worst nightmare. She was home alone, and she had just discovered a burly stranger in their kitchen.

The blonde high school junior screamed at the intruder to get out of their house, but the big brute simply glared at her.

Tawnya quickly sized up the situation and concluded that at five feet six, 125 pounds, she offered little threat to the stranger, who was a six-footer and appeared to weigh well over 200 pounds.

As he began to move toward her, Tawnya was dimly aware of the sound of Burt, her Amazon parrot, whistling for her, just as he always did whenever he heard her come home.

However, on this fateful afternoon, she had much more serious matters on her mind than attending to her bird. She figured that she would soon be fighting for her very survival.

In desperation, Tawnya threw a glass at the intruder, but he easily sidestepped the missile.

As he closed in on her, she managed to kick him in the groin, but he only grunted and seemed annoyed, rather than hurt.

The monster reached out to grab her shirt, and he punched her hard in the ribs.

Later, Tawnya told reporter Susan Fenton that at this point she felt that something too horrible to imagine was about to happen to her.

And then, incredibly, little one-pound Burt was suddenly transformed into a vicious attack parrot. Squawking a fierce battle cry, he flew into the kitchen, landed on the thug's shoulder, and began biting at his neck.

Burt had been her feathered buddy for five years, and Tawnya knew that he was jealous and protective of her, but what could he do against an intruder the size of the creep who threatened her now? She feared for her brave little parrot, because it seemed as though the brute would be able to crush him with one solid blow from his heavy hands.

But Burt had launched a kamikaze attack, and it was obvious that nothing would make him let loose of the lout who threatened his mistress.

Regardless of how the intruder twisted and turned, the enraged parrot could not be shaken loose of his clawhold on his shoulder. And those claws and that beak were drawing blood.

The teenager marveled as she witnessed yet another remarkable transformation. The big, brutish thug became a whining crybaby right before her eyes.

When he finally managed to break away from the world of pain inflicted by the parrot's unyielding beak and claws, he burst out the back door, cursing his bad luck as he ran away.

Satisfied that the intruder had been vanquished, Burt flew to Tawnya, as if to see for himself that she had not been harmed. The grateful teenager could see by his heaving chest that her brave Burt was exhausted from the awful struggle, and she began to quiet him and reassure him that he had heroically saved the day.

Later, Deputy Jim Potter of the Salt Lake County sheriff's office stated that never, in his twenty years of police work, had he ever heard of a bird that went to the aid of its owner.

Tawnya's mother acknowledged that the family had often teased her about the protectiveness of her parrot, but she said that no one would do so ever again. Brave little Burt had saved Tawnya from great possible harm.

*J*udi Bayly of Nashua, New Hampshire, knows for certain that she has a guardian angel, and she knows exactly how it appears to her. Her angel is red-haired with a full-length, furry coat. Her name is Lyric, and she is an eight-year-old Irish setter.

Judi has a breathing disorder and must sleep with an oxygen mask on. One night in the spring of 1996, while Judi's husband was away, the mask slipped off her face as she lay sleeping.

The mask is equipped with an alarm that sounds if such a potentially fatal mishap should occur, and Lyric was immediately alerted to the danger that threatened her owner. The Irish setter tried to awaken Judi, but could not rouse her.

Without hazarding another moment of futile action, Lyric ran to the telephone, knocked off the receiver, and just as he had been trained, hit the button that dialed 911 three times. When the emergency dispatcher at Nashua Fire Rescue answered, Lyric barked into the receiver and an ambulance was soon on the way to the Bayly residence.

Later, doctors stated that Judi Bayly would have died if Lyric had not come to her rescue.

I love all animals, but I guess you'd have to say that I have a special fancy for cats—all cats. On my farm in Iowa, I currently have no fewer than thirty-three cats. They are from all over the world. Some I brought back with me from Ireland, others from the Virgin Islands, still others from California. Each one of the cats has been an orphan in need of a home; and they found a loving home with me, as I consider that cats have always been my best friends and guardians since I was a little girl of three.

Late in December of 1997, I received a phone call from a woman who had lived only about forty miles away from me (I was still living in California at this time). She called to tell me that her house had burned down on December 18, and that she and her husband were alive thanks to their cat. We talked about how our cats have been a source not only of joy and friendship, but of healing, empathy, and protection.

As two cat lovers, we hit it off very well from the beginning, and have remained very close ever since, but Barbara was not calling to complain about the loss of her house and belongings. She was missing her beloved cat, who had saved their very lives.

I knew that I had not seen the cat on my farm, but I rushed right over to Barbara and her husband's place to console her as she told me this most amazing story:

Barbara Kaufman:

In May of 1992, I was awakened by the loud cries of a kitten. It kept on and on, so finally I got out of bed to try and locate where the "meow" calls-in-distress were coming from.

I looked under my bed and all around the bedroom, but I couldn't find anything. The meows continued, and I finally traced the sound to the outside of the house. There by the wall *outside* the bedroom I found this little tiny black kitten that was only about three weeks old—with no mother cat anywhere in sight.

My husband thought I should leave well enough alone for a bit to see if the mother cat would show up. I waited and waited and no mama cat came; so I took on the role of surrogate mom—feeding the kitten we named Arnold.

Months passed and Arnold grew, as we grew more in love with our new family member. One day, while we were remodeling our kitchen, Arnold seemed to find it fun to play in the midst of the disorder and fell victim to a falling board, which hit him smack on the head.

Fortunately, I noticed it right away, and ran to his aid, finding that he was not breathing. I quickly administered mouth-to-kitten first aid, blowing oxygen into his lifeless body. He miraculously came back to me, but the bump on Arnold's little head never did go away.

About a year later, oddly, a mama cat left another tiny little black kitten in the same spot as the first, abandoning it to our adoption. The two cats got along fine and grew up together as brothers. We called our second black kitten Baby.

Both cats guarded my husband and myself as if they were royal Egyptian cats. One would sit at each end of our bed. At the slightest sound, they would stand on their hind legs the way a ferret would. We grew quite used to our two guardian cats at their nightly lookouts at the posts of the bed.

One day in 1996, I was sound asleep when both Arnold and Baby came over to me in my bed and jumped all over me, frantically trying to wake me up. I got up and followed them, as I knew instinctively they were trying to tell me something.

I was led to my kitchen, where both cats jumped up into the bay window and looked out as if to direct my attention there too. I gazed out the window and saw flames rising up to our fence. The fire seemed to be coming from an empty lot next to us, but moving toward us. I ran to the phone and called 911.

The emergency crew came in time to put the fire out, sparing our house, although the fence and part of the yard were damaged. That was rescue number one. Little did we know there was another one to come—one that would prove to be much more dramatic.

That was on the morning of December 18, 1997. My husband and I both had the flu, so I was sleeping in the bedroom and he was asleep in the living room. Our house was a bit on the cold side at night, so we supplemented the heat with a space heater. I had the bedroom lights on very low. I put Baby outside with the other cats, but for some reason, decided to keep Arnold with me.

Even though the cats were "sentinels" at night, Arnold was not that affectionate, so he wasn't that fond of curling up with me. But tonight, I felt that Arnold should be with me—even against my husband's advice that with the flu and all, Arnold should probably be out with the other cats.

On this particular night, Arnold curled up on my chest and just seemed to stare into my eyes for nearly three hours. It was almost eerie, considering what happened later. At about 3:45, Arnold began jumping all over me. He was not only jumping, he was making a loud screeching sound as well.

I jumped out of bed to see smoke filling the room. I yelled out, "Oh, my God, my God!" while running to the living room where my husband was.

The flames and smoke were filling up the house rapidly. We ran back to our bedroom to find that it was totally engulfed in flames. My husband pushed me toward the front door and shoved me out. I ran to a neighbor's house to call 911. I assumed that Arnold and my husband had made it out safely too. After I made the call, I looked back at our house and since I did not see my husband anywhere, I ran back into the house, thinking he must still be inside.

Three policemen grabbed me and fiercely held me down to prevent me from going back into the blazing house. "My Fred, Fred! Please, I have to get my husband out of there!" I cried. I must have been in extreme shock because I was yelling out, "Just let me die with my husband!" But thankfully, the officers held me back.

Numb with fear, suddenly my body went limp, and I was left with the feeling that there was no more life left in me—when I looked up and saw that my husband had been found in the backyard—trying to rescue his truck.

I fell to my knees, and with tears running down my face, thanked God for saving his life. We were both so overjoyed to be alive. Our lost belongings and totally destroyed home paled next to the newfound life in each of us. Fred had burns on his body, some bad, but they did heal. Then we realized that our Arnold, who alerted us in time to save our lives, was missing.

The next day, the newspaper did a story on Arnold saving our lives. It went worldwide on CNN. I remained hopeful that Arnold was still alive, and that all this media attention would locate him. I was thinking that maybe he got scared by the commotion and wandered off.

It was at this point that Barbara called Diane Tessman. Diane went immediately to Barbara's house and to the site of the fire.

Diane Tessman:

I told them, "Arnold made the supreme sacrifice for your lives. Arnold was given to you as a guardian. You saved his life and he saved yours. His role is fulfilled, his mission accomplished. He is where he should be and is happy and loves you and wants you to know that."

Just then, a hawk swooped down over us, and we all felt that this rare event was a confirmation of what I had just said.

Several weeks later, Barbara called me about a dream she had had that Arnold indeed had passed away. She saw him happy in a heavenly place, surrounded by all sorts of other animals.

Barbara Kaufman/
Diane Tessman

Although you might think that a former Green Beret with a fifth-degree black belt in Shotokan karate would not seem to require a great deal of protection, my pit bulls Algonquin and Boadecia saved my life on more than one occasion.

Shortly after I left the Special Forces in 1974, I was hiking the Grand Canyon, intent on viewing the awesome Havasu Falls in the domain of the Havasupai tribe. I had been warned about packs of wild dogs that had been raiding various camps and threatening hikers and campers. I was not particularly worried because I had Algonquin with me, but I appreciated the warning.

As we hiked deep in the canyon, I became aware that we were being stalked. Cautiously glancing over my shoulder from time to time, I was able to count at least six dogs closing in on us.

Algonquin glanced up at me almost indifferently, as if to say, "Don't worry, Tom. I'll handle this."

I freed Algonquin from his leash, then climbed up on a large rock to avoid being bitten.

Algonquin easily fought off all six dogs without sustaining even one bite from their fierce, snapping teeth.

In the period from 1977 to 1980, I spent a great deal of time in a trailer home near Mount Shasta. Because I serve as technical advisor to numerous martial arts motion pictures and personally train many movie stars in the various disciplines, I always make it a point to stay in top physical condition. At that time, it was a part of my daily exercise routine to undertake a daily run to the top of Bear Mountain.

On this particular day, I was running as usual with Algonquin leashed to my waist. Suddenly, he started pulling me off the trail, nearly yanking me off balance. He dragged me almost twenty feet off the trail, barking all the while.

Puzzled by Algonquin's strange behavior, but trusting completely in the pit bull's instincts, I cautiously walked back along the trail.

There were three huge, coiled rattlesnakes behind some small boulders on the path. I would most certainly have jumped over the boulders and landed directly on those deadly rattlers. Somehow, Algonquin had been able to sense their presence far in advance of our approaching them. He had saved my life.

On another occasion some years ago, I had set out on a very steep, one-day climb on a peak in the San Bernardino mountain range with Algonquin hooked to a leash around my hips so we would not be separated. We had descended to the tree level in complete darkness. To my distress, I suddenly found that I had lost my sense of direction.

As a Green Beret, I had always had an exceptional sense of location and direction, but now I had to admit that I was completely turned around.

To make matters worse, cloudbanks arose and totally obscured the moon. I was acutely aware that sheer cliffs with long drops straight down were all around us.

And it was now so dark that I could not even distinguish the trail.

It was growing very cold. I was dressed only in light clothing since I had expected to be back before dark. I knew that it would drop below freezing that night.

It was at that point that a deeper level of my consciousness told me to release Algonquin, to allow him to take the lead. I have an undergraduate degree in Asian religions, and I have learned to listen to my inner direction.

Algonquin led us on what seemed to be a very strange route. We went through brush, around trees, over boulders and logs—but I had the sense that we were going down the mountain.

Algonquin and I walked for two hours, following a completely different route from any that I had ever taken.

Then we followed a dry creek bed for a ways and walked up the bank to emerge directly beside my Jeep. Algonquin had led us to safety.

Tom Muzila

I was only three or four years old on that sunny summer's day when I spotted a badger with its cute "Lone Ranger mask" crawling into its burrow in one of the fields on our Iowa farm. Brimming with the ingenuous confidence of boyhood, I assumed that the creature would surely welcome my company, and I began to crawl in after him.

What I did not understand at that age was that you don't want to mess with a badger under even the very best of circumstances. The badger is a fearless and tremendously powerful animal with sharp teeth and long, deadly claws, and it is always best to give Mr. Badger his own space. You certainly did not crawl into his burrow without an invitation.

With an angry snarl, the perturbed fellow let me know that I was not at all welcome in his abode. And, determined to teach the foolhardy little human invader a lesson in manners and respect for the sanctity of another's castle, the badger roared out of his burrow with every intention of severely punishing me.

I have always had good endurance, but I have never been a fast runner—even with an enraged badger at my heels. My plump little legs could not have outdistanced the belligerent badger for very long, and I would surely have been severely hurt if it had not been for the timely intervention of our old collie, Bill.

Now here is the thing that has puzzled me for years. Bill was really getting up in years, and I don't think that he had enough teeth or muscle left to fight off an angry badger. I have not the slightest doubt that he would have given his life for me, but even his heroic sacrifice would probably not have been enough to prevent the bellicose badger from finishing me off as well.

I can clearly remember Bill distracting the badger from its attack on me—*but I cannot remember where the other two dogs came from.*

Two long, lanky, lop-eared hunting hounds were suddenly there, backing up old Bill, giving the badger what-for. There was no question that Mr. Inhospitable was tough, but now he was out in the open and three big dogs were snapping at him from three different directions. The fight was loud and furious until the snarling badger decided he was getting more grief than he was giving. After each of those big hounds had ripped out sizable chunks of his hair and hide, he wisely chose to scurry up a tree and seek refuge in a branch just out of reach of the snapping jaws of the hounds.

And then, just as quickly as they had appeared to drive the badger away from me, the two big hounds vanished. Our companions in combat gone, Bill and I made an immediate decision to head for home before the badger came back down the tree.

I have thought often of those two mysterious hounds. Our family never owned any dogs other than collies or shepherds, and we never kept more than one dog at a time. My father had a hard-and-fast rule that we never violated: one farm, one dog. It was his decree that to own more than one dog was to invite trouble of the worst kind. Two or three dogs would be more easily tempted to form impromptu hunting parties and slaughter the very livestock that they were supposed to be protecting.

To my recollection, no neighboring farmer owned any dog that even slightly resembled those two lanky, long-eared, baying hounds. Besides, all farmers obeyed the hard-and-fast rule that required all dogs to remain within the confines of their own property. Dogs with an exploratory yen would likely be summarily shot.

Were they strays that just happened to come on the scene of our struggle and jumped into the fray to give old Bill a helping paw? If so, they were unthanked heroes. I know that they didn't come back to the farmyard with Bill and me. They didn't even head for the cattle tank for a well-deserved drink of water. They simply vanished right after they rescued me from that angry badger.

Brad Steiger

I know you probably think that the words *shark* and *safety* don't go together unless in the context of being safe from the shark. But in my case, it was literally a shark that *saved* my family.

When I was very young, my parents would sit and, as they used to say, "talk story"—or, in other words, sit around the campfire and share different personal experiences they had had when they were younger. Mom and Dad told many wonderful stories, but this one has really stayed with me.

I remember my mother telling us that whenever we went swimming we would be protected. When she told me that it was the shark that would protect us, well, that seemed pretty strange. Mother told us that our family "aumakua," or guardian spirit, was the "mano" or shark, and that when we were in the water, should we ever get into trouble, the shark would protect us.

Needless to say, "aumakua" or not, I was not going to make it a point to get real close to any sharks!

Mom told us that the "aumakua" was a serious matter, and to prove that what her family had told her about the shark being their aumakua was true, she described her firsthand experience, one that made her a believer.

A long time before Oahu, Hawaii, became commercialized, when she was just a little girl, she had gone fishing with her cousins and uncle. The fishing was usually better at night, so they all went out in the family canoe for the big catch.

They went out as far from the shore as they could and still be able to see the flicker of light from the lantern left burning on the porch for a marker. Mom's Aunt Tutu, who stayed behind, was sitting there on the porch with the lantern, rocking in her chair and waiting for their safe return.

Mom said that she and her cousins were really having a great time catching fish and playing around. They must have been playing around with a little too much fervor, because the canoe started to rock.

No matter how much Uncle chastised them and warned them about the danger, they kept on, and the boat got to rocking real bad. No one was listening to Uncle or paying attention to his warning, so over the canoe went! When the canoe flipped, everyone went into the water.

The night was extremely dark, with no visible moon, so it was difficult to see. Not only that, but the water wasn't very warm, either.

The first thing was to make sure everyone was there. All were accounted for, so Uncle told them to try to stay together and start swimming toward shore. Well, it's a good thing they could all swim, but not a good thing that they now realized they could not *see* the shore.

In their folly, they hadn't been aware that the canoe had drifted out farther than the eye could keep sight of the lantern. It was so dark that they couldn't tell which direction to swim to head for shore. They were completely disoriented.

Suddenly, one of them yelled out that something had just brushed past her and that whatever it was, was very, very big! Everyone else started to thrash around the water in fear to try and keep away from whatever "it" was. Then one by one, each of them started yelling too because they each felt something swim past them.

Whatever was brushing against them continued, and appeared to be swimming around them in a circle. It continued to circle and circle. By now, everyone was really in a panic, as they knew they were far enough out in the ocean that there could be sharks—*big* sharks.

Uncle tried to regain control and calm everyone down. He told them all to come together and hold hands, forming a circle in the water. Remaining quiet and staying there in a circle must have been quite a challenge when the temptation would be to take off, but they listened and did as Uncle said.

In the stillness, Uncle said he was able to see a fin circling and circling them. Instead of becoming more fearful, Uncle had the sense that something else was happening. He could tell for sure that it was a shark. But each time it would swim around them, it seemed to brush up against them and then do the circle around them again.

The shark continued this behavior, when Uncle finally said, "I think the shark knows we don't know which direction is the shore and he's trying to tell us that he will show us the way if we follow him."

Uncle told all the nieces and nephews to follow him and the shark. I don't think they were ready to believe him, but what other choice did they have?

Finally, they braved it and started to follow the shark, staying as close together as they could in a tight group. They were not being attacked; that became evident. So they swam and swam, following the shark. The shark would swim awhile, then encircle them again to be sure they were all there, and then swim some more, leading the way.

Following this pattern, soon they were able to see that the shark was leading them right—they could see the shore and the flickering light of the lantern on the porch! Then they really bore full speed ahead.

By the time they all reached shore, Aunt Tutu was standing there waiting for them. By now, she knew trouble was brewing and she had been praying for their safety.

Once everyone was safely on land, the shark made one final circle, as if to say good-bye, and off he swam. *That* was when Aunt Tutu told them all that the shark was the family aumakua—and you can bet, they believed her!

Thelma Spencer

*W*hen Silvana Burnett was told by a couple she knew that they would soon be moving away from Edmonton, Alberta, she immediately became concerned about the effects of the move on Freddie, their five-year-old Maltese-poodle mix.

"Oh, we've decided not to take Freddie with us," her friends answered. "It would really not be convenient to have him in our new place. We've decided it would be best to send him to the dog pound to be put to sleep."

Silvana would have none of that. She had always liked Freddie. She made up her mind on the spot that she would become Freddie's new owner. She gave the couple fifty dollars and took the little poodle home with her. She had no idea at the time that it would be the best investment she had ever made.

Just six weeks later, Silvana, who suffers from asthma, was taking a bath when she found herself becoming short of breath. In a few more moments, she began wheezing—and then before she could get out of the tub, she blacked out.

Helplessly, she slipped under the water in the bathtub.

When she regained consciousness, she was spitting soapy water out of her mouth and gasping for breath. And Freddie was jumping up and down on her chest, as if to revive her.

Silvana blinked her eyes in astonishment. The water from the bathtub had been drained. And Freddie held the stopper in his little mouth.

Incredibly, the quick-thinking poodle had seen his new owner slipping under the water and somehow understood that she would drown if he did not act at once. In the next few seconds, the observant dog had jumped in the tub and yanked the stopper out with his teeth, thus allowing the water to escape down the drain and his owner to escape with her life.

Silvana Burnett had been Freddie's benefactor, the person who had saved him from death in the dog pound. He had dramatically returned the favor by saving her from death by drowning.

*K*eeping and riding horses is family tradition with us. My grandfather rode show jumping horses in competition in the 1930s, and I was blessed with having horses around from a very young age.

When I was fifteen, I had one particular mare of which I was really fond. Her name was actually Spud, but I called her Babe. She was small, about 14.3 hands tall (approximately four feet, eight inches), a light reddish brown in color, with four white "stocking" feet and a white blaze face. She was a mixture of quarter horse and thoroughbred and on the spirited side.

Babe just didn't realize that she was smaller than some other horses. She had been used to rope calves, and she had been trained to do so without a bridle—that is, by only leg, hand, and voice cues—when she was two years old. Babe was fast and quick, and she could turn on a dime. If you weren't aware how fast she could turn, you might end up on the ground.

Babe and I became very close. She would do things for me that she would not do for anyone else. If I were feeling downhearted, she would playfully bump me around with her head until I would cheer up. Actually, during my teen years, I may well have spent more time with Babe, riding through the hills, than I did socializing with other kids my own age.

This particular day, I put an old saddle on her with a horn that was probably quite a bit larger than most. We spent an hour or so riding, and when we got back to the barn and I dismounted to remove the saddle, I heard a *buzzz* coming from inside the saddle horn.

Babe and I had been out riding for an hour or so with a rattlesnake in the saddle horn!

We had a lot of rattlesnakes in the central California area where I grew up. And we all recognized that angry buzz the instant we heard it.

I dropped the saddle to the ground, got a stick, and stirred it around inside the saddle horn. There was no mistaking the angry rattle of a creature who didn't appreciate being poked with a stick.

I put Babe in a corral with two other horses; then I got two older cowboys to come back with me to the saddle that I had left on the ground. They shook the rattlesnake out of the horn and disposed of it with a pitchfork.

I know that Babe and I had to have been protected that day as we enjoyed a leisurely ride with our deadly hidden passenger. With her keen senses, she had to have been aware of the snake's presence. Yet she remained calm and cool.

If she had reacted naturally, the way one would expect a horse to respond, she might have spooked and sent me flying to the ground. Considering how fast Babe could move, I could have taken a really nasty fall.

And, of course, not to neglect the obvious, I could have been bitten when I first picked up the saddle, as I rode, or as I dismounted.

There is no question that the angels were watching over Babe and me that day.

Lori Jean Flory, author of
The Wisdom Teachings of Archangel Michael

*P*am and Fred Abma of Ramsey, New Jersey, bought Honeymoon, a potbellied pig, on their wedding trip as a gift to each other. As it turned out, Honeymoon was definitely a gift that kept on giving.

On February 2, 1998, at about 8:00 A.M., according to a story carried by Reuters Limited news service, a fire broke out in the laundry room of the Abmas' home. Fred and Pam were still sleeping, but Honeymoon, now a robust eighteen-month-old one-hundred-pound porker, kept scratching at their bedroom door until they were awakened.

When the couple went to investigate the cause of Honeymoon's persistent bother at their door, they discovered smoke filling the house.

Fortunately, the local fire department quickly extinguished the flames, but the Abmas were pretty disgusted with their two watchdogs, who had slept through the entire potentially tragic event.

There is no question in Pam Abma's mind that it was Honeymoon who had saved everyone's bacon. "She was the only one who smelled the smoke. Our dogs were clueless," she told reporters.

Fred said that he had heard that pigs were very intelligent. Some of them, he commented wryly, were obviously much smarter than dogs. "And it was lucky for us."

I was privileged to enjoy a complete and loving relationship with a German shepherd-Norwegian elkhound mix that I named Ananda, but called Nanda Dog. He was a total love bug, and we entered into an incredibly deep rapport. In addition, Nanda Dog was remarkably intelligent and, for such a large animal, exceedingly gentle.

At the time Nanda Dog was with me, I had a construction business in Oregon. He would come by the site where I was working and bravely climb sixteen-foot ladders to join me on the rooftops of the partially constructed homes.

One time he showed up at a construction site where there were a number of chickens wandering in and out of the work area. I told him that he couldn't even *look* at those chickens.

A little while later, I glanced down at him and saw him looking up at me with pleading eyes. A rooster had perched itself on Nanda Dog's rear end, but he was obeying me and not even looking at it.

Once while we were whitewater rafting, the craft on which Nanda Dog and I were riding capsized in turbulent water. There was a heavy undertow, and I was pulled down. I thought that I would surely drown.

In my flailing about, I could see that Nanda Dog had made it to shore. I was grateful that he would live.

But the strong bond of love that existed between us would not permit him to watch me drown. The big dog plunged back into the river, swam to me, and extended his tail.

I understood his meaning, and I grabbed his tail and allowed him to pull me to shore.

I sat on the bank, telling Nanda Dog over and over that he had saved my life. But he just kept licking my face.

I knew that Nanda Dog felt strongly the call of the wilderness and that there were wolflike impulses within him.

One time when we were driving in a thickly forested area during a night of the full moon, I suddenly had an impulse to stop the van and to get out and howl at the moon with Nanda Dog.

After a brief time, a beautiful silver wolf appeared at the edge of the forest. I knew that the wolf had come to present Nanda Dog with the call of the wild. The two of them left together. I understood.

But I feared for my friend. Things would be different for him in the wilderness. I called for him for over an hour before he returned to me. I hugged him and talked to him. Then he jumped back into the van and fell into a deep sleep.

Dale W. Olson, author of
Knowing Your Intuitive Mind

*O*n his ranch, near Billings, Montana, Jeremy was in the fields rounding up the cattle one day when he noticed what appeared to be an old stray horse running in the distance. Jeremy and Ray, his ranch hand, were each on their faithful horses, and they were very familiar with nearby ranchers and the horses they owned.

"That's something us ranchers keep track of the way some neighbors make it a point to know who goes in what car in the neighborhood and of every new car or trade that goes on around them," Jeremy explained later. "Not really snoopy, more like a neighborhood watch kind of thing."

On seeing the horse, both men gave a silent nod and shrug of the shoulders as if to say, "I don't know anyone who owns that horse—never seen that one before." Their own horses suddenly seemed a bit restless, as if they too had picked up on the unknown intruder horse.

The sight of a horse without a rider was pretty rare near their ranch—in fact, it was pretty rare in any part of the county. Jeremy turned to Ray and yelled, "You keep an eye on the cattle while I see if I can't catch up with that ole gray and see what's up."

Off Jeremy went, riding like thunder to catch up with the old gray. It didn't take him very long, since she appeared to be rather old and not in the best of condition. The gray got spooked and took off, with

Jeremy chasing her. Finally, the gray seemed to be getting too tired to go much farther. Jeremy called to her, "Come on, Old Gray, let me have a look at ya. I'm not gonna hurt ya. I just need to see where you came from. Someone might be missing you by now."

Jeremy got off his horse and managed to gently reach out to the gray. He started petting and stroking her, trying to calm and reassure her. He looked her over for any sign of branding identification marks. Finding none, he said to her, "Well, Old Gray will be your name, if it already isn't, and I guess you'll just have to come with me until I can check out around town to see if anyone knows about you."

He always carried some extra rope with him, so Jeremy fashioned a lead for the old gray and led her back to where Ray was waiting. "Any marks on her?" Ray asked. Realizing that Ray meant I.D. marks, Jeremy answered, "Not a single one that I can find. Let's take her back with us and give her a little kindness while I check around to see what gives."

After about two weeks, not a single person in town or in the surrounding ranches had any idea where this horse could have come from. So Jeremy was given the go-ahead to keep the mare if he chose.

Jeremy kind of took to Old Gray. Somehow, he felt a close identification with her, since he himself had been raised by an uncle and aunt and had spent several years in an orphanage when they were killed in a crash. In some strange way, he felt a strong kinship with this horse and felt good about being able to clean her up and give her some good nutrition. He provided her with some extra supplements to get her in better health.

"You cleaned up pretty darn good," Jeremy said to Old Gray one day as he gave her her daily brushing and a couple of rubs on the head. "And I have to say, I'm kinda glad nobody came to claim you. You and I are family now, aren't we, Old Gray?" He was fully satisfied that she understood every word. "There are folks around who say I ought to just sell you off for glue. They say you're too old and ragged to be good for anything anymore. But heck, they probably say that about me too, behind my back when I ain't lookin'. Pals, we'll just be pals, and pals is good enough for me."

Several months later, Jeremy volunteered to do some repair work on a neighboring rancher's barn and tend to a few chores while the rancher was away on urgent family business. Jeremy drove over to the place in his old pickup, telling Ray and his wife where he'd be and telling them it would only take him several hours.

When Jeremy had been gone for a little over an hour, Ray heard some odd noises out in the barn. When he got out there, he saw that it was Old Gray acting up. She was snorting, kicking up her heels, butting against the corral, and carrying on something terrible. "What on earth is wrong with you, Gray?" Ray puzzled. The other horses were reacting to Gray's uneasiness, and it looked as if it could become a troublesome situation.

Ray tried to talk to Gray and get close enough to her to see what was spooking her or setting her off. "Are you sick, old girl? What is it?" Ray couldn't get close to Gray, who was bucking wildly. Just then, Gray broke the wooden posts and took off out of the barn, racing as if she had a destination in mind.

Ray yelled for his wife Doreen to come out and help, as he was torn between chasing Gray and keeping the other horses from following suit. His wife was out in a flash and took over in the barn while Ray chased after Gray.

There was no way he could catch up with her. He was back in the barn within ten minutes, completely out of breath and panting. "I didn't know she had that much life in her yet—she's gone! I'm going to hop in the car and see if I can find out where she went."

After driving some of the back roads and not finding Old Gray, Ray thought he'd better go tell Jeremy about the bizarre breakout and the missing Gray right away, since he knew how attached Jeremy had become to her.

As Ray pulled into the long drive that led to the ranch where Jeremy was working, he thought he saw smoke billowing from where the barn would be. He stepped hard on the gas pedal. Sure enough, when he got to the barn, it was on fire—and there was Old Gray!

She was going back and forth into the blazing barn. She led Ray to where Jeremy lay unconscious. It was apparent that Old Gray had attempted to drag Jeremy out of the barn with her teeth, biting onto Jeremy's wrangler jacket. She had Jeremy just about out of the barn when Ray got to him.

It turned out that Jeremy had been in the barn pulling on something that was perched precariously above him, and whatever it was had fallen on him hard enough to knock him out. The source of the fire was still unknown, but it *was* very apparent that in not many more minutes, Jeremy would have been asphyxiated. He owed his very life to this Old Gray he had grown so attached to.

"How she possibly could have known that I was in trouble—or even where I was—is beyond me," Jeremy later said, patting her on the head and hugging her hard. "You and me, we'll always stick together, now, won't we, my Gray Beauty?"

Ray offered Gray some sugar cubes, saying, "Thanks, Gray—you not only saved my pal, but you taught me a good lesson too."

As they left the barn, Ray said, "Jeremy, I sure take it back about the 'good for nothin' but glue' comment I made. I hope you'll accept my humble apologies. That gray is worth more than gold. She's quite a treasure!"

I had always believed that Barney, our nine-year-old Saint Bernard, had been short-changed in the brains department. As a Canadian friend of mine used to say about dimwitted folks, Barney seemed a couple of sandwiches short of a picnic.

But my wife Iona and I loved the big brute, in spite of the fact that he was also clumsy and seemingly devoid of all approximations of graceful movement. If we bought a new lounge chair or a fragile lawn ornament, he would be certain to tip one over and break the other before the day was done.

And as a watchdog? Well, if a burglar broke into our place, Barney would probably hold the hoodlum's flashlight in his mouth to provide illumination while he rifled through our belongings.

We had talked about getting rid of Barney and acquiring a dog that would bark at intruders. Barney never barked at strangers, but he raised a ruckus each day when Karl, our mailman for the past ten years, pulled up alongside our mailbox.

"I think Barney believes it's rude to speak to strangers, so he only says 'hello' to the folks he knows and sees every day," Iona figured out one day as we pondered the mystery of why the big fellow only barked at people with whom he was acquainted.

But all the picky fault-finding aside, who was always there to listen to our troubles and to give us a sloppy kiss to cheer us up? Barney!

Who was always at our side when we went for nature walks, bravely keeping tigers and bears away? Why, Barney, of course.

And who was the first to greet us when we returned from work, and the last to say goodnight before we went to bed? None other than our good old buddy, Barney.

One lazy Sunday afternoon in late May, Iona and I were reading the paper when Barney suddenly roused himself from the nap he had been enjoying beside my easy chair. Emitting a strange, loud grunting sound that neither of us had ever heard before from the old boy, he got to his feet and began an urgent pacing that soon focused on the front door.

"He's ahead of schedule," Iona said, "but it's quite obvious that he needs to go out for a potty break."

I took that cool, clinical observation to be my cue that it was I who had been appointed to get up and let Barney out to obey the sudden call of nature.

Once he was in the yard, however, he gave no indication that he was in need of relieving himself. He howled—another thing neither of us had ever heard him do—then began to run swiftly down the gravel road that lay just beyond the small apple orchard at the rear of our property.

I called after him, commanding him to stop—and for the first time in his life, Barney disobeyed me.

Although we lived in a wooded area outside the city limits, the leash laws were very strict in our area. And since I had believed I was only letting Barney out of the house for a quick comfort call, the big guy was devoid of leash and accompanying owner. As a responsible dog owner, I had no choice but to start down the road after him.

Barney ignored all my commands to return to me. He continued running until he ran around the bend forty yards ahead of me and disappeared from my sight.

As I trotted after him, realizing with each labored breath how woefully out of shape I had become, I worried that our beloved Saint Bernard had suffered some kind of mental breakdown.

Then, as I rounded the bend, I was horrified to see a late-model van that had apparently lost control on loose gravel and had skidded head-on into one of the massive oak trees that lined the road at that particular curve.

To my astonishment, I saw that our blundering old Barney had suddenly been transformed into a bonafide Saint Bernard rescue dog. One teenaged girl lay propped against a tree, rubbing her forehead and crying. From the marks and tracks on the gravel road, it was obvious that it had been Barney who had dragged the teenager from the crashed van. As I drew nearer, I could see Barney using his massive jaws and brute animal strength to tug a second girl from the wreckage.

I knelt beside the first girl and saw that the back of her head was bleeding. As if I had the gift of miracle healing, I told the girl that she would be all right. How I wished that I also possessed the power of prophecy—if I did I would have known enough to bring my cell phone with me so that I could call 911 and get immediate help for these girls.

Barney had wrestled the second girl free of the wreckage and was dragging her to rest beside the first teenager. I marveled at those powerful jaws that I had never seen grasp anything bigger or tougher than his rubber rat.

When I looked more closely at the second girl, it was apparent even to my layman's eyes that she had suffered a severely broken leg. She seemed, however, to be in a state of shock that temporarily placed her beyond pain.

"I need to go to call for help," I told the girl with the head wound.

She nodded, grimacing at the pain in her skull. "Just leave your dog with us, okay, mister?"

"Okay," I smiled, stooping down to rub Barney's huge head affectionately. "He is, after all, a Saint Bernard."

"Yeah," she agreed. "They're all trained to rescue people, aren't they? He sure rescued Melinda and me."

"He sure did," I grinned as I turned to run back to the house to call an ambulance and the highway patrol.

Byron M.

For twelve years my husband Paul and I had a black miniature poodle named Toby whom I nicknamed "Shadow" because everywhere I went he was always at my side. We had a bonding between us that was unexplainable. Toby was more than "just a dog."

But one evening when Paul and I returned home a bit later than usual from work, Toby was not there to greet us at the door.

We began at once to search for him—and when we found him it was evident that something terrible had happened, because he didn't have the use of one side of his body. We suspected that he had fallen down the stairs or suffered a stroke, because he couldn't even move his head. We immediately rushed Toby to the veterinary hospital for diagnosis.

Four hours later, we were told that our beloved Toby had numerous physical problems and a disintegrating spine. Vertebrae in his neck had jammed together, making it impossible for him to move his head.

The veterinarian gave us two choices: One, Toby could be kept on painkillers for the rest of his life and placed in an area where there were no stairs. Two, we could have him put to sleep.

The doctor wanted us to think things over carefully before we made a decision, and as I carried Toby out to our car, I sensed that he knew that we needed to spend some time alone.

When we arrived home, I began to receive very clear thought messages from him. He requested that I not lay him in his bed but fix him a place where he could sleep on an angle so his head could lie evenly with his body. As I sat next to him, he communicated that he didn't want me to leave.

The next morning, Paul and I decided that it was not fair to Toby to allow him to suffer, so we made the decision to return to the veterinarian's to have our dear poodle put to sleep.

Toby could move very little, so we carried him inside. As soon as we set him down on the floor in the examination room, it was as if he knew what was going to happen. Incredibly, Toby began walking briskly around in circles. He had a happy face, and his tail was wagging.

Paul and I left the room knowing that Toby's pain would soon be over. I was also acutely aware that I would be lost for a while without my best friend.

As we walked to the car, Toby came through to me in a profound thought message. He was free! He was free! He no longer suffered pain, and I received an impression of his spirit soaring, as if he were a lamb leaping over the clouds.

And then I received an extraordinary message from Toby's spirit: *"One day in the future, you will receive a telephone call from a woman moving out of the state. She will not be able to take her one-year-old silver-gray poodle with her. She will request that you take him. When the call comes, you are to pick up the dog—for I will be returning to you in that dog's body!"*

One morning in March, nearly seven months after Toby's death in September, a woman telephoned me and explained that she had been given my name by the Humane Society. She went on to say that she was in the process of moving out of state, and due to housing restrictions in her new home she would not be able to bring her one-year-old silver-gray poodle with her. She could not understand her feelings, but somehow she just *knew* that I was to take her dog.

She wasn't interested in selling him. He was a registered poodle, and three people had said that they wanted to buy the dog—but she knew that none of them were to have him. Her only object was to find him a good home. She asked if I could come pick him up that evening.

My first reaction was one of disbelief. Toby's prediction had been fulfilled to the letter.

I contacted Paul and told him that we were going that night to meet an "old friend."

The woman greeted us with Joey tucked under one arm. As soon as we had exchanged pleasantries and sat down on the sofa, she put him down on the floor and he immediately jumped up on Paul's lap and wasn't about to move. After receiving information about Joey's likes and dislikes, we departed with the poodle clinging to Paul.

As soon as we arrived home and set Joey down in the foyer, he started checking out the house. Minutes later, he scurried up the stairs, heading for our bedroom.

He leaped on our bed and quickly tunneled under the blankets to the foot of the bed—exactly where Toby used to sleep.

As we observed all of Joey's antics the rest of that evening, there was no doubt in our minds that Toby had indeed returned to us.

The next morning when we opened the back door so Joey could have his morning run, we noticed something very unique about the way he ran. *He moved like a lamb, leaping over clouds!*

It was an incredible sight to see.

Joey has been with us for four years now. He sticks to me like glue. Although he doesn't speak to me telepathically as Toby did, Joey has no difficulty letting me know exactly what he wants. Joey is proof that dogs *don't* die. Their spirits live on.

Beverly Hale Watson, author of
Reflections of the Heart

*T*he DeGraffenreid brothers had certainly not planned on their small fishing boat sinking on that late spring afternoon in 1990, and they only had water-ski vests to keep them afloat in the turbulent, shark-infested waters of Channel Islands National Park off the Southern California coast. Daryl told Gary that he would swim for an island several miles away in an effort to bring help.

As he swam, Daryl noticed that he had attracted the attention of a baby sea lion. After a few moments, the little guy came so close to him that the two made direct eye contact.

Daryl suddenly had the seemingly crazy thought that rather than simply kibbitzing, the sea lion could go for help. When the creature continued to stare at him, Daryl suddenly found himself shouting, "Go get some help!"

He may have felt momentarily ridiculous for telling his troubles to a baby sea lion, but he had to wonder if it was only his imagination when the little fellow turned and quickly swam away—just as if it had truly understood that the human struggling in the water needed some big-time assistance.

Daryl lifted his head above the waterline for a moment and saw that he really did need help. Sharks had begun to circle him.

And one of them was monstrous. He estimated that it was more than twenty feet long.

Daryl was getting weaker by the second. The swells kept coming at him, and he was going under each time. He was beginning to lose consciousness. And the sharks were circling closer and closer.

Then, miraculously, fifteen to twenty sea lions suddenly appeared to form a wall of protection around him.

Knowing that sea lions themselves were a favorite meal for sharks, Daryl marveled at the bravery of these creatures that had created a living barrier between him and the toothy sea marauders.

Somehow, the combined forces of such a large number of sea lions managed to drive the sharks away. But in spite of the bravery of his marine benefactors, Daryl found himself steadily sinking beneath the waves as his ski vest became increasingly waterlogged.

But as he later told reporter Marie Terry, God must have had something very special in mind for the DeGraffenreid brothers, for just then a Coast Guard boat with Gary on board arrived to pull him out of the sea.

In reviewing the remarkable case of the band of sea lions that gathered to save Daryl DeGraffenreid from a shark attack, park ranger Don Morris said that while it was common for curious sea lions to swim up to humans in the water, he had never before heard of an instance wherein the sea-dwelling mammals had banded together to assist one of their landlocked cousins.

My liberator of the spirit came to intervene at a time when my life was filled with sadness and despair. He came to guide me, to fill me with love, and to show me the path of endurance and spiritual growth.

In June of 1986 I sat in an old rocking chair—my prayer chair—in our bedroom in Pennsylvania and begged God to let me die. Although I had always been strong in my faith, despair and utter helplessness had filled me for weeks, and I could not seem to surmount those negative feelings. A family situation that had existed for years and seemingly could not be resolved had enveloped me in new, even more painful ways—and I was about ready to give up.

Even though I was only in mid-life, I had reached the point where I no longer wished to live. It took a supreme effort of will to force myself to choke back the tears and decide to face life, regardless of how painful its sorrows might be.

Two weeks later, my husband Bob, my youngest daughter, and I stopped in a small shopping mall in Rochester, New Hampshire, on our way to our lakeside cottage. I was immediately drawn to a man and two children who sat on a round bench with a carton before them and a sign above them that proclaimed, *Free Kittens*.

Throughout the years, Bob, our six children, and I had enjoyed many wonderful pets, but we had never had a cat. Bob had always refused to allow cats into our house because of his own negative feelings toward them. This had been a great sadness to me, for I had always had a good relationship with my pet cats from my childhood and teenage years until I married.

On that summer morning—without even looking at the kittens in the carton—I knew in my spirit that one of them had to be mine.

With such a *knowing* within, and with undaunting persistence that seemed supernaturally charged, I relentlessly refused to accept Bob's dissenting vote. With what could only have been divine intervention, he suddenly uttered the "yes" that I had hoped to hear for thirty-two years. With all the stresses of our family troubles, my heart danced for the first time in ages.

By this time only one kitten remained in the box— and that little fellow, I knew, was for me. That morning in that mall, God's gift of love took the form of a tiny marmalade and white kitten about eight weeks old. I believe that God knew how desperately I needed a guide and an Earth angel—one that I could hold in my arms and that would help me release my tears as I buried my face in his soft fur.

I accepted that indescribable gift of love, and in so doing, from that moment on, I have felt the Lord's love to me more powerfully every day. I believe with a certainty beyond comprehension that this beautiful creature is a heavenly being in the form of an animal.

I gave him the dignified name of Rochester, after the town in which God brought us together. Exactly twelve years later, he is ever at my side — or on my lap or desk — as I write. His love and constancy fill me with joy and imbue me with spiritual wisdom, compassion, and a healing of heart, soul, and spirit. His presence is steadfast and unwavering as we share our moments, days, and years together.

In September of 1986, I went to our cottage to make a retreat. For a city girl, this was a big step, for I had never gone alone into the woods. Rochester's companionship gave me the courage to experience an unforgettable week of solitude with him — praying, learning, reading, writing, and discovering the path of healing. This retreat was written down and later became a book. Rochester was ever with me as I wrote, inspiring me to create a work that would help others who suffered similar family stresses. That book, published in 1991, continues to minister to families in need of such guidance.

It was only one of numerous books that Rochester inspired me to write. A newly published work is one that confronts the senseless cruelties that thoughtless humans may inflict upon innocent and sentient beings. It was Rochester who alerted me to the rights of animals and who taught me about *Ahimsa* — nonviolence, non-killing. As a result, in 1989 I became a vegetarian, as did Bob, who had long since been won over by Rochester's winning ways.

And while those family problems still exist, I no longer long to die because of them. I have been forever changed by one of God's little four-legged miracle workers. Now I wish to realize the exquisite beauty of the sacrament of each moment.

Two years ago, Bob, Rochester, and I moved permanently to the cottage on the lake. We abide here in joy. Rochester and I are even writing a new book together.

Janice Gray Kolb, author of
Compassion for All Creatures

From the moment she entered our home she captured our hearts, this eight-pound ball of fluff with a heart as big as all outdoors.

She was a Shih Tzu puppy, and I had gotten her because my husband was going out of town for two weeks and I did not want to be alone.

Charity, our Pekingese, had been gone for a year and a half. She had been twenty years old when I finally put her to sleep after a long illness.

I had been on my spiritual path for quite a while and had reached the place where I felt God was really dealing with me about unconditional love. So I prayed to Him that this little dog would be my teacher, and I named her Bhakti Rose.

Bhakti is a Sanskrit word meaning unconditional love and devotion. Little Bhakti Rose filled our empty nest, and she helped heal our sick marriage. No matter what the situation, she could always bring a smile to our faces and make everything a little better.

I had been trying to work through bouts of depression for most of my adult life, but Bhakti Rose soon had me out for walks and chatting with everyone in town. I was steadily feeling better.

Children would come to the door for Bhakti to come out and play fetch with them. At night, after a full day, she would stretch out along the arm of my recliner and just love me.

Bhakti Rose had her own playpen right beside our bed. I realized that she loved little stuffed animals, so a toy box became necessary.

She went where we went. If the weather was nice, she waited in the car. If she did have to stay home, it was never for more than three hours, or she went to my daughter's to be baby-sat.

Often she went to work with me and then waited for me to take an exercise class. She would take one of her stuffed babies, and everyone would talk to her as they went in and out of my office.

When we went to our favorite little restaurant, we sat where she could see us and wait for her grilled chicken breast.

Bhakti Rose made friends wherever she went. One couple took six pictures of her and decided that it was time for them to get another little dog to love. Bhakti made dog lovers out of people who had never liked dogs.

She had only one bad habit—and that wasn't really bad because her motivation was pure. About once a month she would run off to see her friend Amos, who, poor dog, was always kept on a chain at his dog house. Amos's owner would invariably call to complain that our dog was in his yard, but before I could get up there,

Bhakti Rose would be on her way home with her little ears flying in the wind.

She had made Amos's day a little more interesting— and she had given his grumpy owner something to complain about. Her work was never done.

One evening Bhakti Rose went to work with me and then we picked up my husband to go to dinner. When we got home, my purse strap got caught on something under the car seat. The interior light was not working, and in the darkness I did not realize that she had slipped out of the car.

My husband had gone into the house, and something told him to come back outside to see where Bhakti was. Her usual routine was to go beside the house to relieve herself, then make a mad dash into the house to get her doggy bag.

But when I called for her, she was not around. I looked across the street to the field and saw her running home.

At the same time, a car was coming down the street.

It was as though I was frozen in a bad dream—and everything was happening in slow motion.

I screamed when I heard the sickening *thump*, and when the car got past, there she lay.

Bhakti tried to get up three times, and then she left us.

We thought our hearts would break.

We put Bhakti Rose into a nice box with her favorite babies—a duck she had gotten one Easter and a Tweety

Bird that she had picked out herself at Fall Festival. We placed her in her playpen beside our bed one last night.

The next morning our family and some neighbors came and cried with us. One son-in-law dug the grave and another cleaned up the blood. One daughter brought flowers.

We put concrete slabs over the grave and surrounded it with a little fence. I would plant flowers around it in the spring.

Bhakti Rose was unconditional love personified. She was patient, gentle, long-suffering, not easily provoked. She bore all things, endured all things, and she was kind.

She loved us when we ignored her because we were busy or tired. She loved us when we had morning breath and when we were too interested in other things to take her for a walk.

Approximately two weeks before she passed over, Bhakti Rose did something unusual. She licked the psoriasis lesions on my palms for maybe five to ten minutes. Ordinarily I would have stopped her, but it somehow reminded me of Jesus washing the feet of his disciples. I knew that she was ministering to me in the only way that she could.

Bhakti Rose left two beautiful pups that are with my daughters, and they visit nearly every day. It will be sad to see them wrestling in the yard and playing with Bhakti's toys, but they are a part of her legacy and we love them.

Several days before Bhakti died, my daughter dreamed that we were at Virginia Beach, and Bhakti and her pups were playing as usual. Puzzled, she saw that Bhakti Rose kept leaving the two puppies to run off and be with a dog that did not seem to belong with the group.

Then she realized that Bhakti was greeting Charity, our old Pekingese.

Early one morning when I was praying and releasing Bhakti back to God, I asked for a sign of some kind just to let me know that she was okay. I said that I would not specify what kind of sign I would look for, but just for the grace to know it when I saw it.

At that exact moment, a drop of water hit my closed eyelid and rolled down my cheek just like a tear.

I looked up to see if the roof was leaking. It was not—nor had it been raining.

I looked down, and there on the floor was a single water-drop.

I have seen Bhakti Rose three times since she passed over. Once in the twilight I saw her in the yard, looking in the window as she used to do when she was ready to come in. Once, again at twilight, I saw her on my bed.

But the clearest was one morning very early. I had just finished my meditation, and after giving Devotee, my new dog, orders to stay, I went into the bedroom.

When I came out, there was a little dog so happy to see me, swishing around my feet.

Annoyed with the energetic puppy I assumed was Devotee, I looked down with the scolding words, "I told you to stay . . ."

The words died on my lips, for there was Bhakti Rose! And then she was gone.

A few nights later, I dreamed of her—and she was so tiny I could hold her in one hand. I believe she was saying goodbye.

Bette M. Goodson

$\mathcal{P}$*rofessor* William Serdahley, who teaches health sciences at the Montana State University Department of Health and Human Development, told writer Esmond Choueke of a most incredible and unusual near-death experience of a seven-year-old boy.

One afternoon, seven-year-old Pete and a friend had gone fishing off a bridge. According to the friend who had accompanied him, Pete was casting his line into the water when he lost his footing and slipped. He fell into the river below. He must have hit his head on a rock as he plunged into the water, and he was rendered unconscious.

By the time the friend was able to find help and get back to the bridge, Pete had been submerged at the bottom of the murky river for some five to ten minutes.

Every minute seemed like an hour as they attempted to find Pete's body. Fortunately, it did not take long for an adept policeman, who moved into action quickly to locate the body in the muddy river. The officer retrieved the body and brought it up to lie flat on the river bank.

The hope that Pete would somehow still be alive was doused when it was discovered that he had no pulse at all and that his respiration had completely ceased. By all appearances and indications, Pete was dead.

But attempts to revive Pete were miraculously successful. Pete later told Professor Serdahley that something amazing happened to him when he drowned. Pete said that he was floating in a very special kind of place. He explained that he had never been to this place before, and he described it as tunnel-like. He said that he became somewhat frightened as he floated and drifted deeper inside this tunnel.

"Then I saw my old dog Andy and my old cat Abby come over to me in the tunnel," Pete said. "I was really happy to see them, because I hadn't seen them since they died—a long time ago."

Pete said that Andy and Abby were just as nice as he remembered them. His fear lifted, and he began to feel a lot better knowing that his beloved pets were there with him. He explained that he no longer felt alone and frightened.

Pete's dog Andy came close to him and started licking his hand. "I began petting him," Pete said. "Then he put his head right by mine and began to lick my face."

That was when Pete was brought to life, at the same time, he said, that he was waking up "in the hospital with people all around me."

Pete was examined thoroughly and carefully by a number of doctors. Even a smaller amount of time without breathing could have caused severe brain damage, in spite of his being revived. But he was found to have no permanent damage, mental or physical, from his near-death experience at the bottom of a muddy river.

Professor Serdahley expressed his opinion about Pete's amazing experience, saying that "when Andy the spirit dog licked his face, it was a signal that Pete should return to his body. Andy was telling him it wasn't his time to die yet."

Thousands upon thousands of men and women have discovered, to their benefit in well-being and improved health, that interacting with animals can have a profound healing effect on the human body, mind, and spirit. And medical science agrees that our pets can truly become four-legged physicians that can bring good health into our lives.

Doctors Prescribe Pets for the Sick

As early as 1860, in her *Notes on Nursing*, Florence Nightingale, the British reformer of hospital nursing whose very name has become synonymous with the healing principle, advised her readers that a dog provided an excellent companion for the sick.

And now, over a hundred years later, numerous medical studies have demonstrated that owning a pet can slash your risk of heart disease, lower your blood pressure, and reduce your cholesterol levels. In general, pet owners have significantly reduced levels of known risk factors for cardiovascular disease.

The Amazing Healing Powers of Pets

A 1991 University of Pennsylvania study of heart attack victims showed that owning a pet can mean the difference between death and recovery. Medical researchers found that simply stroking the fur of a cat or dog can reduce blood pressure and heart rate. The rhythmic process of petting Fido or Felix can have the same effect on a stressed-out patient as certain relaxation techniques, including meditation and biofeedback.

Dr. Leo Bustad of the College of Veterinary Medicine at Washington State University has expressed his disappointment that it has taken so long for some people to understand the full value of pets in improving their health and mental attitudes. In his opinion, the very presence of pets seems to enhance patients' ability to block pain.

A survey conducted by Dr. Erika Friedmann of Brooklyn College revealed that the survival rate for heart patients who have pets is much higher than that for patients without animal companionship.

Owning a Dog Can Lower a Man's Cholesterol

At an international medical conference held in Montreal in the summer of 1992, Dr. Warwick Anderson of Australia's Baker Research Institute announced findings that demonstrated that male owners of dogs had significantly lower levels of blood triglyceride, cholesterol, and systolic blood pressure. In his analysis of more than five thousand male patients, Dr. Anderson found that dog owners had "significantly reduced levels of known risk factors for cardiovascular disease."

Petting your pooch—or any other pet, one might assume—also stimulates a soothing sensation of well-being. Such a response, researchers believe, is one of very ancient origin, derived from the relaxing ambiance achieved during the process of mutual grooming that our human ancestors performed on one another.

And veterinarians have known for years that a dog's heart rate and blood pressure drop dramatically when it is stroked or petted, so we now have scientific proof that beneficial results are attained for both you and your pet when you pause in your daily tasks to scratch your dog or cat behind the ears.

Pets Reduce Our Tensions Better Than Our Best Friends Can

In a series of revealing tests, Dr. Karen Allen, associate professor in the School of Medicine at the State University of New York at Buffalo, assigned forty-five women the task of solving a series of brain-teasing arithmetic problems that were especially designed to produce stress and tension. Some of the women tackled the problems with their dogs with them in the testing room. Others performed the difficult assignment in the company of a human friend. Both groups of women had their blood pressure, skin response, and other body functions monitored while they worked on the tough arithmetic puzzlers.

Interestingly, body responses remained normal among those women who toiled with only their dogs present. On the other hand, those women subjects who had a human friend at their side showed dramatically increased physiological responses. Even the presence of a very close, supportive human friend caused the women who labored over the arithmetic problems to have increased blood pressure, a rapid pulse rate, and sweating palms.

To suggest why this might be so, Dr. Allen pointed out that we know very well that our dogs love us unconditionally and don't judge us or seek to evaluate us. And they certainly couldn't care less how well we might do on an arithmetic test.

Even though the friends of the women subjects who sat next to them made no comments and offered support through eye contact and posture, their very presence caused the women being tested to demonstrate an increase in blood pressure, pulse rate, and other physical expressions of stress and tension. Remarkably, just knowing their friends were at their sides made the subjects more likely to rush through the problems and make mistakes.

The results of the tests clearly demonstrated that the mathematical brain-teasers were solved with greater ease and fewer mistakes by the women who were accompanied by their dogs.

Pets help us to keep our mental equilibrium when it seems as though the very world is crumbling down around us. In times of stress they very often make us laugh and help us avoid taking life too seriously.

And in those instances when we know full well that we have truly screwed up and made a mess of things, our pets' nonjudgmental presence seems more welcome than that of a well-meaning friend who reminds us that he or she told us that such and such would surely happen. Dr. Allen herself admitted to journalists that she could think of many special situations when she would rather be with her dog than with other people.

Getting a Pet Can Save a Marriage

Researchers have conducted tests that determined that quarrelsome, combative couples, who were nonetheless attempting to save their marriages, became less tense and angry when a dog was in the room with them. The same couples were also much more successful in discussing the true nature of their marital differences when a dog was present.

Dr. Alfred Coodley, a clinical professor emeritus of psychiatry at the University of Southern California School of Medicine, has said that having a dog can improve marriages, regardless of whether a couple is unhappy and having problems or very much in love and supportive of one another.

In his opinion, the very fact that petting a dog can significantly lower blood pressure, heart rate, and muscular tension can permit individuals to feel calmer and better able to handle problems that might arise in their marriage. The less stress that exists between spouses, the more effectively they are able to talk openly about any matters that might otherwise breed disagreement and tension.

Pets Are Essential to Happiness for Folks Over Fifty

A nationwide survey of six hundred men and women over the age of fifty discovered pets to be essential to happiness.

Fifty-seven percent of those surveyed by Carol Morgan of the Strategic Directions Group, a Minneapolis-based marketing firm, said that their pets were very important to their quality of life.

People Live Longer If They Have a Pet

Researchers at the University of Pennsylvania found that elderly heart patients live much longer if they have a pet to keep them company.

In general, it has been demonstrated that dog owners seek medical care an amazing 21 percent less often than people who live without canine companionship.

Dogs Can Predict the Onset of Epileptic Seizures

At the annual congress of the British Veterinary Association held in Torquay, England, in September 1991, one of the world's leading veterinarians verified reports that there were many documented cases on record of dogs accurately predicting an oncoming epileptic seizure in their owners—even before their owners themselves perceived the first indications of an episode. Andrew Edney, president of the World Association of Small Animal Veterinary Organizations, stated that dogs had been so successful in detecting oncoming seizures that there was enormous potential in establishing studies to identify future "predictor" dogs for use as companions for epileptics.

In the spring of 1993, the *Veterinary Record* published the results of a survey of thirty-seven dog owners conducted by Edney in which he determined that none of the dogs in the sample had been formally trained to respond to their owners' seizures. Drawing on their own inner resources, twenty-one of the thirty-seven dogs often appeared restless or apprehensive prior to the onset of their owners' seizures, and twenty-five of them made dramatic attempts to attract attention to their owners once a seizure had begun.

Those who speculated as to how untrained dogs could so accurately predict the onset of their owners' epileptic seizures theorized that observant and sensitive canine companions can somehow sense the bioelectrical disturbances experienced by humans undergoing an epileptic episode.

Other researchers suggested that epileptics may emit a characteristic odor prior to a seizure. Although such an odor may be undetectable to other humans, it is noticed by the more sensitive noses of their dogs.

Elizabeth Rudy, a veterinarian from Seattle who is herself an epileptic, is made aware of an oncoming seizure by her golden retriever Ribbon. If they are indoors and Ribbon senses that Elizabeth is about to have an epileptic episode, he will come to her, lick her hands, and stare at her. If they happen to be outdoors, Ribbon will stop walking and lower his ears.

Reina Berner, executive director of the Epilepsy Institute in New York, spoke of a patient who at one time was afraid to leave her home because her seizures caused her to fall. Suddenly her dog seemed to develop the ability to sense an imminent attack, and he would begin to bark frantically until his owner sat down. After her dog had demonstrated his remarkable talent for sensing an epileptic episode, the woman was able to leave her home, secure in the knowledge that her four-legged physician would be certain to warn her of an impending seizure in time for her to ready herself for its onset.

Dogs Appear to Sense the Subtle Signs of Hypoglycemic Coma

Many insulin-injecting diabetics insist that their dogs can detect sharp falls in their blood sugar in sufficient time for them to ingest carbohydrates and thus prevent themselves from slipping into a hypoglycemic coma.

Researchers suggest that in cases where dogs have detected their owners' approaching hypoglycemia, the animals may have been close enough to their humans to have reacted to sudden changes in body temperature experienced by the diabetic. Other theorists have said that the diabetic may emit a certain odor accompanying the subtle chemical change in the body.

Dogs May Detect Skin Cancer by Smell

Dr. Hywel Williams, a staff physician in the dermatology department at King's College Hospital in London, has theorized that melanomas might emit a particular odor that sensitive dogs might be able to sniff out.

Among the recent cases that have given rise to Dr. Williams's provocative theory is that of forty-seven-year-old Bonita Whitfield, who was alerted to a serious skin cancer by Baby, her mixed-breed dog.

According to Bonita, whenever she was walking around in the privacy of her home wearing shorts, Baby would start to whine and attempt to bite her on the thigh.

Because she knew her Baby only as a gentle dog who had never before made a move to bite anyone, Bonita was baffled by her behavior, and she scolded her many times—until she noticed that Baby appeared to be after only a particular mole on her thigh. Bonita had never really paid any attention to it because it was toward the back of her thigh and out of her normal range of vision.

But it was this mole and this mole alone that Baby seemed determined to nip out of her flesh.

Intrigued enough by Baby's persistent attacks on her thigh to visit a doctor in order to have the mole examined, Bonita soon found herself at King's College Hospital undergoing surgery for a malignant melanoma. Thankfully the surgeons were able to inform her that they had been able to excise the cancer from her body before it had spread.

There was no question in Bonita Whitfield's mind: Baby had saved her life by pestering her about the mole.

Fascinated by Ms. Whitfield's dramatic account of her dog's preternatural ability to detect a malignant melanoma, Dr. Williams announced his intention to initiate a study that would investigate whether or not certain sensitive dogs really could detect skin cancer in their owners. If the study proves to be successful, there may well be a place for four-legged physicians in a screening process for malignant melanomas.

*W*hen the elderly man shut the door in his face, it seemed as though their last chance for rescue had been taken from them. The raging blizzard had caught them unprepared, their car was stuck in a ditch, and attempting to walk any farther for help in the darkness and the blinding snow seemed futile, foolhardy, and fraught with danger.

Carter Allen and his girlfriend Dawn had stayed out late one night not long after New Year's Day 1996, and because it had begun snowing heavily, they decided not to head for home, but to drive only as far as his mother's house in a rural area near Walker, Minnesota.

But by then the heavy snow had become a full-blown blizzard, and when they tried to negotiate a deep snowdrift, their car slid sideways into a ditch. They were stuck, with no choice but to walk for help.

The fierce storm mercilessly drove the stinging snow into their eyes, and the windchill was well below zero. They soon realized that their tennis shoes, jeans, sweaters, and jackets offered little protection against the cold and the swirling, blinding snow. Carter led Dawn back to the shelter of the car, but he decided to go alone in a desperate attempt to find help.

In what seemed nightmarish torture, struggling through knee-deep drifts, trying to keep his mind off the terrible cold, he had come at last to a farmhouse —

only to have the frightened old man within refuse to help them.

While trudging back to the car, Carter was only dimly aware of something following behind him, but he was too numb from the cold and too exhausted to make the effort to turn around and investigate. Later, he would remember offering a brief prayer for help before he saw only blackness and felt himself falling.

As he struggled to regain consciousness, he became aware of some prickly, hairy form covering him like a blanket. As his senses cleared, he saw that a large black dog had stretched itself on top of him.

"Good boy," Carter thanked the huge animal. But then he wondered if the dog were wild. Surely no one's pet would be out in such terrible weather.

"I looked into his eyes," Carter Allen wrote in the January/February 1997 issue of *Angels on Earth*. "He seemed somehow to *want* to help me, almost as if he *knew* why we had crossed paths."

As the dog allowed him to press his face into its fur and breathe the air warmed by its body, Carter thought that he had never before seen such a magnificent animal — nor had he seen a breed similar to this massive canine.

Carter rose to his feet with renewed strength and plodded slowly through the snowdrifts, back to the car where Dawn awaited him. Although he had expected the dog to return with him, his dark rescuer had disappeared back into the storm.

As he and Dawn huddled close in the shelter of the back seat, Carter told her of his encounter with the black dog that had saved his life. Just the recounting of the experience seemed to warm him and to help Dawn relax in his arms.

Early the next morning, the driver of a snowplow rapped on their window, freed them from their makeshift igloo, then drove them to Carter's mother's house.

Mrs. Allen was startled to learn that Dawn and her son had been out all night in the awful blizzard. God must have been watching over them to preserve them, she said.

When Carter added that God had been aided by a large black dog, his mother stated that there was no such dog being kept in any of the places on her road. She was certain of that.

But on two occasions, she added, she had seen a large black wolf wandering around the very spot where Carter had fallen.

Whatever his dark angel was, Carter concludes, dog or wolf, he knows that it wasn't just wandering about in the storm. It had been sent to him in answer to his prayer for help.

It isn't often that cats and dogs will put aside their centuries-old grievances and combine efforts for a common goal, but it does happen—and a lot more often than popular folklore, comic strips, and animated cartoons would have you believe.

In 1995, Dick Kristofferson grew weary of big-city life in Milwaukee and decided that he could just as easily conduct his work as a freelance illustrator from a much smaller town in Wisconsin's heartland. After all, it was the electronic age. Fax machines, computers, and e-mail would permit him to be just as effective away from the hustle and bustle, and would allow his wife Priscilla and himself to rear their two kids in the small-town atmosphere that they themselves had enjoyed so much as children growing up in rural Michigan.

They were fortunate enough to be able to manage the down payment on a classic old farmhouse about two miles outside of a town of about 6,000 population. Although the barn had long since been torn down, there were still a number of outbuildings in good enough condition to serve as storage areas and a playhouse for their son Andy, ten, and daughter Angie, seven. There was a small shed near the garage that would serve as a comfortable dwelling place for Freya, their terrier, even after her expected litter of pups arrived.

Dick had named the dog after the Norse goddess and because they had gotten her on a Friday, Freya's day. The little terrier took as quickly to rural life as the kids did.

Shortly after the Kristoffersons completed their move, it appeared for a tense moment or two that there might be a battle royal over territorial rights to the old corncrib on the place. Andy spotted an extremely large black female cat preening herself in the open doorway of the building, and the big lady appeared confident that the corncrib belonged to her. Strangely enough, however, the large cat and the pregnant terrier seemed to take to one another immediately. There was not one growl or hiss to be heard as the two became acquainted with one another.

The Kristoffersons learned that the cat belonged to their neighbors, Carl and Mary Johnson, but that it had accustomed itself to frequenting the place they now occupied. "It was kind of like she was keeping an eye on the place while it sat empty for those many months," Mary said. "If she bothers you, just shoosh her on home."

In the view of Andy and Angie, the big cat was just another welcome playmate. No need to "shoosh" her on home.

The Johnsons had given her the elegant moniker of Cassandra, but the kids nicknamed her Ninja, because of her black coat and her ability to move quietly and stealthily through the trees and tall grasses. Sometimes they called her Pepper in contrast to Freya—Salt—who was nearly all white with the exception of a couple of brown patches.

The whole family got a kick out of watching Ninja grooming Freya, lovingly licking her coat, cleaning her ears, "washing" her tummy with her rough little tongue.

Priscilla suggested that Ninja probably planned on being the midwife when it was time for Freya to birth her pups.

Two weeks after their move, Freya delivered four pups in the old corncrib that had appeared to be Ninja's favorite haunt. And, yes, the big cat was there to see that everything went as smoothly as might be hoped.

A couple of nights after the pups had arrived, the Kristoffersons went to town to see a movie. Andy and Angie were reluctant to leave Freya, insisting that she was still kind of weak and woozy from having given birth so recently, but they fixed a nice bed for her made up of some tattered blankets that had been used in the move.

"There," Priscilla teased, "Freya is as comfortable as anyone ever made me after I gave birth to you two little monsters."

When the family returned home around ten o'clock, they were horrified to see Freya outside the corncrib, staggering as if from exhaustion. In the illumination of the headlights, they saw splotches of blood staining her white coat.

Angie started crying and would have run to Freya at once if Priscilla hadn't caught her arm, instinctively perceiving that something was very wrong with the picture they were seeing before them.

The Kristoffersons had little time to puzzle over what had happened to their terrier. Something came running out of the shadows toward Freya.

Growling angrily, the little dog rose to meet the threat and was sent sprawling into the long grass near the corncrib.

The thing that had attacked Freya scampered off into the shadows, but Dick was able to glimpse it long enough to be able to identify it in the illumination cast by the yard light on the garage door.

"It's a big muskrat," he said. "It's come up from the creek after the pups. I've got to go inside and get my shotgun."

But the muskrat had regrouped and was charging Freya in another savage onslaught.

Dick had no time to get his shotgun, and he was too far away from the corncrib to attempt to chase the creature away. And this time Freya was easily knocked aside, appearing to collapse in exhaustion.

The muskrat had free and open access to the tender flesh of the pups.

That was when another shadowy figure rose from the doorway to meet head-on the determined charge of the hungry muskrat. The predator emitted a loud squeal of pain as it caught the raking slash of claws across its nose.

"It's Ninja," Andy cried out. "She's come to help Freya and the pups."

It was true. The big black cat reared back on its hind legs, poised like an experienced prizefighter, jabbing and thrusting at the huge muskrat with drawn claws.

Ninja's delaying tactic had given Freya time to regain her breath and her balance. She jumped the muskrat from behind and sank her sharp terrier's teeth into the intruder's neck.

The muskrat shook off Freya's charge, ran about seven or eight feet into the darkness, then came running back for another try at the puppies.

It met a solid wall of cat fur and stiff terrier hair. The three combatants rolled in the grass, growling, hissing, spitting, biting, clawing, squealing.

The muskrat was big and tough and mean—and it was determined to feast on fresh meat. But Ninja and Freya were equally determined that it would not dine that night on those newborn puppies in the corncrib. And it was obvious that they intended to fight to the death.

The muskrat retreated once more into the darkness. Freya was panting heavily and appeared ready to drop from exhaustion. Ninja hissed her defiance after the scavenger.

"Oh, no," Angie and Andy screamed. "Here comes the muskrat again!"

Freya tried valiantly to regain her feet, but she seemed down and out. Ninja left her side to stand in the doorway of the corncrib ready to defend her friend's babies.

But the muskrat never reached the doorway. Dick had run inside and grabbed his shotgun. The 12-gauge birdshot slammed into the muskrat and lifted it two feet into the air. When it crumpled to the grass, it lay still, its legs twitching their final movements. Freya and Ninja made certain the monster was dead.

Later, when Dick inspected the area outside of the corncrib, it was apparent that the battle had raged for hours. The manner in which the grass was torn up outside the building indicated that Freya must have caught the scent of the muskrat approaching and knew full well the purpose for the critter's nocturnal visit. Although she was still weak from having so recently given birth, she positioned herself outside the crib to keep the invader away from her pups.

Ninja had either heard or sensed the struggle and the terrible predicament that her friend was in and had come charging over from the Johnsons to help Freya defend her puppies. From the claw marks on the doorstep, it was clear that the big black cat had planted herself right there to prevent the muskrat from entering the corncrib. If it hadn't been for her feline reinforcements, it was likely that Freya would have lost a pup or two before the Kristoffersons returned from the movie.

The next morning, Dick took both Freya and Ninja to see the local veterinarian. Fortunately, neither of them was seriously injured, but they were given precautionary shots in case the muskrat was rabid or carrying other diseases.

Dick and Priscilla yielded to the kids' entreaties and kept Freya and her puppies on the front porch for the next few weeks until they were larger and more able to defend themselves from nocturnal marauders.

And, as might have been expected, "Aunt" Ninja came over every day to inspect the progress of her little spotted niece and her three all-white nephews.

*P*it bulls generally get a bad rap in the media. And there is no denying that some careless and irresponsible dog owners have allowed their pit bulls unrestrained license and uncurbed freedom that, in turn, have given the breed some really bad press as vicious and aggressive animals. Responsible owners who carefully observe leash laws and proper training methods and who exhibit a loving, caring attitude toward their dogs universally report that pit bulls have a gentle and compassionate nature.

Skeptics may take note of the accomplishments of Weela, a pit bull terrier, who seemed to accept a month-long mission to rescue people and animals during the disastrous floods that ravaged Southern California early in 1993.

Among Weela's heroic deeds were such courageous acts as the following:

~ She waded across a raging river to carry a heavy backpack of food to stranded dogs.
~ She guided a rescue team around quicksand, thus enabling them to rescue starving horses.
~ She sensed a deadly undertow at the edge of the Tijuana River and prevented thirty Mexican men, women, and children from entering the water to cross at that point.

~ She located frightened dogs and guided them to high ground.

~ She dragged human rescuers free of mud when they were stuck and unable to move.

Weela's owner, Lori Watkins of Imperial Beach, California, speaks with great pride of her rugged female pit bull. She points out that Weela had never been trained in any rescue techniques—it was as if she simply knew what to do.

Once Ms. Watkins sank into mud up to her waist. At first Weela tried to dig her out; then she just grabbed her owner by her coat and pulled her out. Pit bulls, Ms. Watkins observed, are incredibly strong animals.

When the floods finally subsided, grateful residents of the area tabulated that the sixty-five-pound, four-legged superhero had saved the lives of thirty humans, twenty-nine dogs, thirteen horses, and one cat. Weela was subsequently named the winner of the Ken-L Ration Dog Hero of the Year award.

*T*he strange, star-crossed romance between eleven-foot, two-thousand-pound Wilma the whale and Rocky the husky dog probably hasn't lasted, but in 1993, according to tour boat operator Jim Johnson of Chedabucto Bay, Nova Scotia, it was love at first sight between the two mismatched mammals.

Wilma, an orphaned beluga whale, first swam into the bay after her mother had been killed. From the very onset of her sojourn in the bay, she had been very friendly with local residents, but the minute she first set eyes on Rocky, she seemed to fall in love.

Rocky was on board Johnson's boat, gazing into the bay, when Wilma spotted him.

"She started circling the boat," Johnson told writer Burt McFarlane. "Then she swam beside us, got on her tail so her head was out of the water—and she was just sort of 'standing' there, looking at Rocky."

Human onlookers couldn't help being amused as they observed Wilma turning her head from side to side, staring at Rocky with one eye at a time, making clicking and whistling noises out of her blowhole.

And then, to everyone's astonished delight, Rocky leaned out of the boat and rubbed noses and cheeks with Wilma. After that first "kiss," according to residents of Chedabucto Bay, the surf and turf twosome repeated their little love ritual dozens of times.

On one occasion, Rocky couldn't resist the impulse to jump into the bay to join his whale of a girlfriend.

Wilma poked around at the husky, and he at her. Onlookers described the two as seeming as happy as two pups falling over each other.

Inevitably, other whales enter the bay from time to time to come calling on Wilma—but at last report, she appeared to be true to Rocky, and she had refused to leave the bay with others of her own species.

When three-year-old Jennifer wandered away from the family farm near Cowetta, Oklahoma, in October of 1994, her parents, Deborah and Lee Johnson, tried to keep themselves from visualizing the worst.

All night long, while the Johnsons and hundreds of volunteers searched for the little girl, they could hear the howls of ravenous coyotes echoing across the fields.

The only thing that gave the Johnsons courage and maintained their expectation of a miracle was their belief that their loyal dogs, Moose and Muley, were with Jennifer.

The next morning when the searchers found Jennifer safe and unharmed, they gave thanks to a benevolent providence and to the faithful watchdogs Moose and Muley. The mute evidence of dozens of tracks indicated that coyotes had encircled the frightened toddler and her two loyal bodyguards all night long. But it was equally clear from the tufts of fur and drops of blood that Moose and Muley had not allowed any of the marauders to cross the line to harm their little mistress.

*A*t first Lily McDermott could not understand why Boo, her 143-pound Newfoundland, was acting so excited about a log bobbing up and down at the base of a waterfall on California's Yuba River.

She had Boo on a forty-foot leash, and three times the big dog had tried to head upriver, then turned back as if to tell her something. All Lily could see up ahead was a churning waterfall and a dark shape swirling around in the whirlpool.

And then that one particular "log" that had so captured Boo's attention suddenly sprouted an arm clutching a red gas can.

Immediately Lily slipped the leash off Boo, and he raced away over boulders and dove into the water. As his concerned owner watched the remarkable drama being played out before her, she saw the stalwart Newfoundland swim upstream and dive into a whirlpool.

"He dove under again and again," she told journalist Paul Bannister. "The fourth time he went down, I thought my dog was dead. Then up bobbed Boo's big black head—with the man's arm between his jaws!"

But it wasn't over yet. Boo had saved the man from the downward suction of the whirlpool, but now the current had them, pulling them downriver through two rocky patches of white water.

Somehow, through all the struggles in the choppy, swiftly moving river, Boo managed to hold the man's head above water.

Boo and the man he had saved from drowning finally made it to shore about eighty yards downstream.

When she reached them, Lily discovered the answer to her puzzlement over why the drowning man had not been calling out for help. He was a deaf-mute.

Later, the rescued man, Link Hill, a gold miner, wrote that he had been crossing the turbulent river with a gas can in one hand when he lost his grip on a rope that stretched from bank to bank. Tumbling backward, he struck his head on a rock and was pulled over a six-foot waterfall into the whirlpool. Because he was a deaf-mute, he couldn't call for help, and people hiking along the riverbank seemed unable to see him.

Lily McDermott admitted that she had not seen any of the travails of Hill and would have hiked on oblivious to his predicament if it had not been for Boo.

"If Boo hadn't spotted me and come to my rescue," Hill wrote, "I would have drowned."

Boo's act of courage was recognized by a commendation from the Newfoundland Club of America and by the presentation of a special hero award from the Gaines dog food company.

*W*e have spoken over the years to many individuals who claim to have received some kind of miracle after close interaction with a dolphin. Few cases are more dramatic than that of little Katie Philips, who was literally transformed from a "hopeless vegetable" to a happy, productive child after a swim with a dolphin named Squirt.

In 1991, Beverley Allitt, a nurse in Great Britain, went on a tragic, murderous rampage that resulted in the death of four children and the maiming of nine others. She gave Becky, Katie's twin sister, a fatal injection of insulin. Then, for whatever unimaginable reason, Nurse Allitt decided to crush nine-week-old Katie to death.

Somehow Katie survived; but in addition to suffering five broken ribs, she was clinically dead for forty-two minutes and her brain was deprived of oxygen for that same length of time. Medical experts informed her parents, Peter and Sue Philips, that while one of their twin daughters had lived through the vicious attacks by Nurse Allitt, she would be a hopeless vegetable for the rest of her life.

But the Philipses refused to give up hope. For one thing, they had read about the remarkable achievements of dolphin therapy, and they decided that they had nothing to lose and everything to gain by visiting the Dolphin-Human Therapy Center in Key Largo, Florida.

Katie was two years old when they were accepted into the dolphin program and managed to obtain the necessary funds to travel to the center. Their daughter was unable to walk or even to crawl. She couldn't talk, sit up, or feed herself.

But the moment Katie met Squirt, all those terrible troubles began to fade. She was permitted to swim in the pool with the friendly dolphin, and it was obvious by her smiles that she was responding to Squirt's aquatic charms.

That night, back in their room, Sue Philips placed Katie on her back on the floor. To her parents' immeasurable delight, she rolled over onto her stomach, pushed herself up on all fours, and began to crawl for the very first time.

Rejoicing in their "dolphin miracle," but forced to return to England because of their budgetary limitations, the Philipses managed to raise enough money to return to the Dolphin-Human Therapy Center a year later. On that occasion, Katie's swim with Squirt prompted her to stand unassisted, then swim across the pool to her father's arms.

When the Philips family returned to England this time, Katie was able to attend a special school near their home in Grantham. According to her parents, little Katie now walks freely wherever she wishes, talks nonstop, and asks endless questions. In their opinion, their child's swim with a dolphin brought about the miracle that gave Katie the will to achieve.

As we said, we receive so many accounts of similar "dolphin miracles" that we must wonder what marvelous linkup there must be between humans and their sea-dwelling cousins.

For years now, marine biologists have been telling us that dolphins share numerous traits with our own species, including intelligence and congeniality. Then, in August 1998, researchers at Texas A&M University stated that the genetic makeup of dolphins is amazingly similar to our own.

In point of fact, thirteen of twenty-two dolphin chromosomes are exactly the same as human chromosomes. Of the remaining nine dolphin chromosomes, many are combinations or rearrangements of their human counterparts. Three dolphin genes were also identified by the Texas A&M University researchers as similar to human genes.

This means that we have more in common with dolphins than with such land mammals as dogs, horses, cattle, or pigs. But it would seem that the human-dolphin connection responsible for such miracles as that of the astonishing recovery of Katie Philips has more to do with a spiritual, rather than a physical, connection.

"*Tony*, help me! Please help me!"

Eighty-three-year-old Sara Pizzo cried out for help, hoping desperately that her neighbor, Tony Kypreos, would hear her cries and come to her assistance.

It was a sad and peculiar accident. Sara had fallen off her porch while trying to reach her newspaper on that spring morning in 1997. She called out for help at once, but no one could see her behind the thick bushes in front of her house. She had pushed her medical alert button many times, but apparently it wouldn't work outside.

Sara had lain there helplessly for hours before Tony came out of his house to go to work.

"Tony, help me . . . please," she called out once again. But after so many hours of crying for help, her voice had been reduced to a faint whisper.

Her heart sank. There was no way that Tony could hear her. He would get into his car, start the motor, drive off to work, and not be home until after dark. What would become of her in all that time?

In desperation, she tried to cry out for help as loud as her strength would allow: "Tony . . . it's Sara. Help me!"

Then a small miracle occurred. Tony's dog had run out to the driveway to see her master off to work. And fortunately for Sara Pizzo, Tony Kypreos is so proud of his purebred boxer that he named her after himself, "Toni."

Toni's ears pricked up when she faintly heard what she believed to be her friend Sara calling her name. Toni liked Sara, because the elderly woman was always slipping her tasty little tidbits of food.

Tony, help me . . . please.

Toni sensed that there was something not quite right about Sara's voice. It sounded weak, and she sensed that her friend was somehow in distress.

Toni caught at her owner's pant leg as he was getting into his car.

Kypreos was startled. "Toni, bad girl! Where are your manners? You've never done such a bad thing before."

Later Kypreos said that he feared his beloved Toni had gone berserk. She started dragging him across the yard and wouldn't stop.

And when she wasn't tugging at him, she was barking her head off.

Try as he might to quiet her and order her back into the house, Toni just wasn't accepting any commands that led her away from Sara Pizzo, who was lying helplessly only a few yards away behind a clump of bushes.

Kypreos was becoming increasingly frustrated and upset with his normally superbly mannered boxer. Every time he tried to head back to his car and drive off to work, Toni renewed her efforts to pull him toward the fence that separated his yard from Sara Pizzo's.

And then at last, dragged over to the fence once again for the umpteenth time, Tony Kypreos finally spotted his elderly neighbor lying on the ground.

In spite of her nightmarish ordeal, Sara Pizzo suffered only minor cuts and bruises. "I kept yelling for Tony," she explained later to reporters, "but it was always Toni, his dog, who was coming to save me. She could hear my tiny little voice calling for help."

Toni, the ninety-pound heroine of the day, was later honored at New York City's Essex House at a lunch sponsored by the American Society for the Prevention of Cruelty to Animals.

Cyril Jones, a resident of Nantmore, Wales, told a most interesting story of animal–human interaction to the *Daily Telegraph*, August 27, 1996.

In 1942, when he was a sergeant in the British military service, he parachuted into Sumatra along with scores of other soldiers who had been given the desperate mission of holding up the Japanese advance across Southeast Asia for as long as possible. Crashing down through the thick jungle growth in his parachute, Sergeant Jones became separated from the rest of the men—and to make matters worse, his parachute became tangled in the branches of a tree, and he was unable to cut himself free.

Jones hung there suspended for an agonizing twelve days, dangling helplessly above a mass of jungle vegetation. He would surely have starved to death if it hadn't been for a monkey that seemed to understand his plight. Somehow the agile native of the jungle perceived that the human in the strange, swinging harness was unable to escape the straps and lines that imprisoned him in the tree.

Jones remembered vividly how the little fellow befriended him and regularly brought him food. "Most often bananas, but sometimes he would bring me bamboo shoots and he showed me how to eat them."

When he finally managed to cut himself loose from the parachute, Jones found that the monkey had grown so fond of him that it insisted on following him.

Unfortunately, Jones went almost immediately from his imprisonment in the tree to capture by the Japanese, who placed him in a prison camp.

Remembering that his loyal simian benefactor had followed him to the camp, Jones said that he had to force the monkey to leave, because it would attempt to defend him and begin to attack the Japanese soldiers whenever they sought to bully him. Although it saddened him to send the monkey on its way, he could not bear the thought of the soldiers shooting it.

Cyril Jones survived the difficult days in the Japanese prison camp and made it back to his native Wales after the war. He thinks often of the monkey that befriended him and kept him alive for those twelve days while he hung from the parachute. But, he added, it was a long time before he could think of eating bananas again.

*O*ur dog Queen was one of the most incredibly rich and complex personalities I have ever known. She will always remain in my memory as an entity who was as individual and unique as any human being with whom I have become friends and shared deep and meaningful experiences.

Perhaps it was because she had come into the world as a pup running free in the woods, with a wild collie for a mother and a wolf for a father, that she was able to share our rough farm life as a sovereign entity who always demanded that she be accepted as an equal on her own terms. In our years together, Queen worked with us, defended us, nearly froze to death in blizzards with us, and loved us unconditionally without holding back an iota of her energy.

But never as a "pet," never as "only a dog." Always as Queen, an individual, independent being, who was our friend, our partner, our coworker, our full-fledged family member.

Let me tell you how we first met.

I was nine years old that spring of 1945 when a terrible plague of distemper struck the dogs in northwestern Iowa. We were a farm family that tilled 280 acres of cropland and kept fifty head of cattle, about two hundred pigs, and a couple hundred chickens, and we desperately needed a dog. Because of the distemper, we lost a couple of pups before we even had a chance to name them.

Farmers in those days really had to rely on a dependable four-legged troubleshooter to keep things running smoothly. Even if they could afford to hire a decent, hardworking, two-legged hand to help with the seeding, cultivating, and harvesting of the field crops, farmers still needed to have a loyal dog to herd livestock and to bring the cows home for evening milking.

And after dark, when the bone-weary farmers were getting their sleep, their dreams were made more peaceful by the knowledge that their alert dog was standing watch, keeping those crafty foxes and cunning civet cats away from the chicken house, discouraging rascally raccoons from stealing the maturing ears of corn, and dissuading wild dogs from molesting the calves and small pigs.

Before the awful distemper plague hit the countryside there had been no shortage at all of folks trying to give puppies away at county fairs, beside gas stations, and outside of grocery stores on Saturday nights. Now dogs were as hard to come by as white crows or two-headed calves.

One day a farmer who supplemented his income by trapping minks, muskrats, and foxes along a creek that ran through a thick stand of woods told my father that he had come upon a wild collie and her litter of pups about a month before. When he had sighted them more recently, there was only one pup remaining.

"If you folks really need a dog so bad, you might try catching that wild dog's pup before someone shoots the both of them," he said. "Folks around here would rather shoot a wild dog than look at it."

That night at the supper table, Dad brought up the matter of the wild dog and her pup for family discussion. Under ordinary circumstances, farmers like us would never have considered bringing a wild dog within a mile of our place. We'd have shunned a wild dog even more than a fox, a coyote, or a wolf, because a dog that has broken free to run wild on its own will be smarter and meaner and more destructive than any canine of a species that has never been domesticated.

For instance, wolves will kill only what they need to survive, and they usually single out only the old and the crippled from a herd of deer, moose, cattle, or sheep. But wild dogs most often kill just for the fun of it, the sport of it—perhaps not unlike the human masters from whom they have fled—and they may leave twenty or more slaughtered sheep or a dozen mutilated cows and calves for a horrified farmer to discover during morning chores.

Dad brought up other arguments against our attempting to corral the wild pup. With a wolf for a father and a wild dog for a mother, the pup just might be impossible to tame. We might be bringing a killer home to watch our livestock.

It was also solid folk wisdom to get a pup as young as possible. This one could be as much as four to six months old. And it already had been raiding henhouses and chasing cattle. It might already be too set in its ways to ever stop killing livestock.

But the bottom line was always the same. We really needed a dog.

So with the full understanding that we might never be able to fully domesticate the offspring of a wild dog, the next afternoon just before chore time, the four of us—Dad, Mom, my five-year-old sister June, and me—set off for the section of the woods where the trappers and farmers had most often seen the outlaw collie and her pup. We were joined at the edge of the forested area by the trapper, who volunteered to help us in our quest.

Although we tried to be as quiet as possible in our approach to the wild dog's lair, the big white collie emerged from her hiding place and watched us cautiously as we approached. She barked a couple of high-pitched warning yelps, and her pup crawled out from a dug-out area under a fallen tree. And then the dogs made their move, running off into the woods.

I still don't know how we did it, but after what proved to be an endurance race through the trees and brush, our winded, panting group somehow managed to win our prize when we cornered the pup against an old rusted wire fence. Although a mother dog will fight to the death to defend her young pups, this mama must have considered her offspring old enough to fend for itself, because she kept right on running without looking back to determine its fate.

Dad pulled on thick leather work gloves, then took off his belt and looped it around the dog's snapping jaws. None of us wanted to be bitten—especially by a dog that had never had rabies or distemper shots.

Mom and Dad were not at all pleased with their immediate inspection of the struggling dog at the end of his belt. It was older than they had hoped—probably six months—and it was a female, which meant it could soon produce a litter of its own.

The trapper offered to shoot it. "You'll probably never be able to train her," he said soberly. "She will probably eat your chickens and kill your pigs."

But after several minutes of serious deliberation concerning the young female dog's ultimate fate, we decided that our desperate need for a dog surpassed all other considerations and overrode all negative possibilities. We thanked our trapper friend for his help; then we wrapped the snarling, struggling dog in the Indian blanket that we always kept on the back seat of our old Chevy, and we carried her with us to our farm.

The first week was terrible. We had to keep her locked up in the old building near the house where we kept the corncobs we used in our cookstove. It seemed as though she never stopped snarling and snapping at us. She went for days without eating.

And then, whether it was resignation to her fate or starvation that got the better of her, she began to accept the food that we offered her. But not the touch of our hands. I received a painful bite to my fingers when I tried to pet her.

After she settled down enough to be freed from the cobhouse and it appeared that she was accepting her new environment as her personal territory, it was time to name her.

I don't think we ever considered calling her anything other than Queen. From the moment she began to survey her new kingdom, her haughty, imperious, no-nonsense manner proclaimed her to be a majestic sovereign entity.

One of the first major breakthroughs came with Queen's dog license and collar. Since it appeared that she would become domesticated enough for us to keep her, we had to license her to distinguish her from the packs of stray and wild dogs that were anathema to farmers and their livestock.

Queen would now endure a friendly pat or scratch every now and then, but to attempt to scold her for a misdeed or an inability to follow a command would only prompt a snarl and a warning growl in reply. When Dad first approached her with the collar, Queen showed her teeth and backed away.

And then Dad started telling her in a cheery and enthusiastic voice how pretty she would look in the collar.

In my nine-year-old wisdom, I looked at Dad in wonderment. How could he think that a dog—a wild one at that—would understand the concept of "pretty"?

"Come on, kids," he encouraged June and me. "Tell Queen how pretty the collar is. Tell her how spiffy she'll look when she wears it."

We joined Dad's chorus of seduction and began to sing the praises of the magnificent leather collar with the ornamental metallic studs and the license tag in the key ring. Strangely enough, Queen began to express some curiosity toward the collar.

To my complete astonishment, she ceased her snarling and allowed Dad to fasten the collar around her neck. Oh, boy, I thought, here we go! As soon as she feels the snugness of the leather band around her throat, she is going to go crazy.

It never happened. Queen actually seemed to preen, to strut back and forth in front of us.

With Dad's prompting we all chorused how pretty she was with her spiffy new collar.

From that day on, it was impossible to touch that collar under any circumstances. To attempt to remove it in order to trim her hair during the hot and humid Iowa summers was out of the question. Even playfully suggesting that one might want to borrow her collar would invite a warning growl.

If her acquisition of the beautiful collar was a breakthrough in terms of Queen's growing acceptance of domestication, one night a couple of weeks later forcefully demonstrated her acceptance of her love for us and her desire to become a permanent member of our family.

Dad was in town attending a church meeting. My sister and I were asleep. Mom was waiting up for Dad, but she had dozed off in front of the radio when she was awakened by the sounds of barking and growling outside by the barn. Without hesitation, our fearless and impulsive mother went to investigate.

Queen was standing her ground in front of the stockyard fence, snarling, growling, somehow managing to bluff back a marauding pack of five dogs from entering the area where some newborn calves huddled next to their mothers. Queen was not a small dog, but neither had she inherited the size of her collie mother or her wolf father. What she lacked in bulk she made up in wiry strength and fierce aggressiveness, but she was dwarfed by most of the wild dogs she was doing her best to face down.

As Mom drew nearer, she had a sense of a kind of inner struggle going on within Queen's psyche. It was as if she were tempted to step aside and join in the pack's slaughter of the calves. It was as if the call of the wild were wrestling with her growing sense of loyalty to a farm family and trying its best to pin it to the ground.

But when a large German shepherd lunged forward to jump over the fence and get at the calves, Queen savagely blocked its leap and knocked it to the ground. The big dog cowered back for just a few moments from the much smaller defender. Then, together with two other pack members, it charged Queen with vicious snarls and snapping teeth.

Three against one was too much for Mom. She charged into the fray, launching powerful kicks into the ribs, haunches, and heads of the dogs that were tearing at Queen's throat.

The invaders backed off long enough for Queen to get to her feet. Mom shouted at Queen to follow her, and the two of them began a desperate run for the house, where Dad kept a .22 rifle in a closet for such nocturnal marauders.

And then two very angry, savagely snarling dogs were blocking Mom's path, unwilling to allow her to escape.

But Queen had caught her second wind. She attacked the two much larger dogs with such fury that they went yelping away in painful retreat, followed closely by the other three mutts, who decided they didn't want to be left alone to face such determined defenders of the calves.

When Dad returned home, he scolded Mom for having charged out into the darkness and into the midst of a vicious dogfight.

Mom's reply was simple and direct. "Queen was defending the calves against five wild dogs. They had her down and they would have killed her. I had to save her life. I got the dogs off her, and we were running for the house. Then Queen ended up saving my life. Those dogs would have got me down and probably tried to rip open my throat if she hadn't turned into a tiger and driven them off."

Dad and Mom knelt and both of them hugged Queen. The once wild dog had made her final decision. She was now a full-fledged member of the family, ready to lay down her life for any one of us.

Fifty years later, I remain convinced that love is the greatest force in the universe and that it flows as powerfully among animals as it does among humans.

And when it comes to dogs, well, for some time now I've visualized the following little vignette from the dim, gray mists of prehistory.

It's anywhere from 12,000 to 20,000 years ago. An intelligent, essentially pragmatic, and especially hungry wolf stands just beyond the ring of light cast by a campfire on a particularly dark, wet, and cold night. He catches the sour scent of humans; he knows the fear of fire; but he also inhales the tantalizing smell of meat cooking over the glowing coals.

He considers the situation. The hairy two-leggeds are slow, clumsy, and weak. They have no claws, and their teeth are too short to be any real threat. But somehow they have acquired the awesome magic of fire, and they possess the unique ability to throw rocks and sticks with their forepaws, often with dangerous accuracy.

They make sounds that appear somehow meaningful to others of their kind, and they very often work together as if they were one body and one mind. When they do this, they can conquer the greatest and fiercest of other creatures.

In addition, the wolf senses a certain kinship with the creatures huddled around the fire. The humans gather in packs, as wolves do. They have family units, as wolves do. They appear to have a sense of loyalty to the pack, just as wolves do. Maybe wolves and humans are brothers and sisters on some level of spirit.

Perhaps, the wolf speculates, we can work together. After all, I possess skills and abilities that the two-leggeds lack. They have hardly any sense of smell, they have very little endurance, and they move with scarcely any speed at all. And I possess a most magnificent howl and bark. I could track game for them, warn them of the approach of lions, tigers, and bears. . . . And, oh, my, does that meat cooking over the coals ever smell good. Hey, you two-leggeds, I'm coming in. Can we talk?

Although I have undoubtedly taken considerable literary license with the interior monologue of my intelligent, pragmatic, and hungry wolf standing at the edge of a prehistoric human camp, I believe that it was in some such manner that a remarkable social and spiritual contract was established between human and canine that has endured unbroken for thousands of years. Somewhere along the pathway of evolutionary development for both species, the ancestors of today's dogs bade farewell to the kingdom of their fellow four-leggeds and decided to throw in their lot with *Homo sapiens*. We humans have been much the better for the arrangement.

Brad Steiger

*D*o animals have souls? Will there be animals in heaven?

While it is not the purpose of this book to resolve such weighty cosmological questions, we cannot help but point out that if we humans could demonstrate the kind of unconditional love of one another that our animal companions have shown toward us, think what a planet of peace and harmony we would inhabit.

If, as the Bible tells us, the Creator fashioned our kind to be just a little lower than the angels, were our pets created just a little below us?

But if, as the wise and holy teachers have admonished through the centuries, to err is human and to forgive divine, then it would often appear that our animal companions have moved a step or two ahead of us on the path of spiritual evolution.

In speaking of the passing of a beloved dog, Lori Jean Flory, coauthor of *The Wisdom Teachings of Archangel Michael*, once told us that she knew dogs went to heaven, because they are angels in disguise.

Does the presence of animal ghosts prove that there is a spiritual essence within them that survives physical death?

In his intriguing and well-documented book *Pet Souls: Evidence That Animals Survive Death*, Scott S. Smith recounts numerous stories of men and women who saw the ghosts of their own physically deceased pets.

"From 1991 to 1993 I asked readers of a couple of dozen magazines about animals or the supernatural to send me any experiences they might have had that would have bearing on the question [of animal immortality]," Smith writes in his preface. "I was impressed by the variety and complexity of the reports. Skeptics who believe that such things can be dismissed as wishful hallucinations will be surprised at the collective strengths of these stories. . . . There are also the cases of multiple observers. . . . It is difficult to shake the conviction that the deceased pets which were encountered were in some form really there."

To cite only one of the many stories that Smith recounts, there is the experience of I. L. Heiberg of Wisconsin, who told of Trusty, a German shepherd who had lived with his family for fourteen years. It was with great sadness that the Heiberg family was forced to euthanize the old dog when they moved to Portland in 1941.

During the spring of 1945, when they were back visiting in Wisconsin, they decided to stop by their former home. Heiberg said that he was sitting in his father's pickup truck when he looked out the side window and saw the image of Trusty, as plain as could be.

"Her tail was wagging and her front feet were on the truck running board, and she was looking up at me with a big doggy welcoming grin on her face," he stated.

Mindful that his mind and his memories might be playing tricks on him, he looked ahead out the windshield, then back again to the running board—and Trusty was still there.

When he told his mother of his sighting, he learned that his brother had also claimed to have seen Trusty. He stated that the German shepherd had "bounded towards him with a happy grin on her face, tail wagging."

His brother had seen Trusty as if she were transparent, and he had asked their mother to keep his sighting a secret. But when the two men compared notes, neither could accuse the other of being crazy.

At the time of their respective sightings, I. L. Heiberg was thirty-one and his brother was twenty-nine. "So we were old enough to be certain of what we saw," he concluded.

*I*n her fascinating book *Animal Talk: Interspecies Telepathic Communication*, Penelope Smith makes a point with which we wholeheartedly agree: "One of the major barriers to receiving communication from animals is allowing your own thoughts, distractions, or preconceived notions to interfere. You need to be quietly receptive to what animals wish to relay."

You Must Maintain an Attitude of Calm to Achieve Rapport with Your Pet

Brad first observed the essential truth that one must maintain an attitude of calm when communicating with animals when he was just a boy on the farm and was given the chore of herding cattle or pigs. He noticed that if he stayed calm and confident, the majority of the livestock would move in an orderly fashion, and in this same tranquil mental state, Queen, Brad's wolf-collie mix, seemed to be able to read his thoughts. Without his saying a word, Queen would move directly toward the occasional straying animal and remind it that it was part of the herd.

If, however, Brad grew nervous and uncertain that he could adequately fulfill his burden of responsibility, the pigs or cattle would begin to act spooked. Queen would become almost hyperactive, as if she were forced somehow to compensate for her young master's feelings of inadequacy. She would begin to bark and to snap randomly at members of the herd, punishing them cruelly for no particular reason.

If Brad should then begin to shout at Queen to stop her from biting the animals, she would become even more aggressive toward the herd. She would react to the diminishing element of calm in Brad's increasingly nervous mind and would respond only to the chaos that was growing ever stronger within his psyche.

If Brad totally lost his self-control, Queen would revert to the wild dog that his family had captured in the woods as a pup and begin viciously to attack the animals. And the more Brad panicked, the more savage she would become.

And then there would be a stampede. Perhaps not on the scale that you may have seen in western movies, but large enough to scatter the pigs or cattle throughout the corn and soybean fields, destroying fences and crops wherever they ran. And serious enough to put both Queen and Brad in the doghouse for the next few days.

The Close Union of Traditional Native Americans with All of Nature

The traditional native people of North America maintain a particularly close sense of union with all of nature and all of its creatures. Today's practitioners of Native American Medicine power retain strong links between the human and the nonhuman occupants of the Earth.

If you truly wish to communicate with your pet, then you must also respect that animal as a sovereign entity who has joined you as a companion on your Earth walk.

The more you permit yourself to become one with your pet, the more aware you will become of the world of nature around you. You will begin to feel that you are a part of a much greater and larger reality.

And as your awareness grows, you will find yourself developing the ability to reach beyond your physical body and tune in on an intelligence that appears to fill all of space.

The more you eliminate the old, rigid boundaries that have been erected between human and animal and allow yourself to experience the oneness of all life, the greater you will find your ability to communicate with your pet — regardless of the physical distance that may sometimes separate you.

Establishing a Mindlink with Your Pet

Whenever you sit quietly in meditation, you are achieving at least some level of attunement with the blessed harmony that governs the universe. Every time you spend even a few minutes in the silence, you are helping to undo the ancient lies and restrictions that separate you from the Oneness of all life and from completely and harmoniously blending your consciousness with that of your pet.

Try this exercise in achieving a mental linkup between you and your pet.

Sit down facing your pet. Do not speak.

Look at your pet's face for at least one or two minutes. Even if you feel that you have looked into those beautiful, loving, soulful eyes a thousand times before, look into them anew and search their infinite depths.

Truly become aware of your pet's personal features. Notice the various colors and textures of its coat. Study the shapes and characteristics of its snout, eyes, teeth, ears, and so on.

Is there any aspect of your pet's face or other features that seems to attract you or intrigue you more than any other?

Try to imagine what your pet is thinking.

Try to visualize how *you* look through your pet's eyes.

What aspects of your personal appearance do you think most attracts or intrigues your pet?

If you have noticed that your pet has seemed troubled about something lately, try to receive an impression of what it is that has been causing it stress. Are there any images that seem to be moving into your consciousness? If so, focus on those images.

As you focus on those images, pay close attention to whether they in any way make you feel tense or nervous, excited or anticipatory.

Continue to observe your pet closely. Does he or she seem to be acting tense or nervous, excited or anticipatory? Your pet may be transmitting thought-images of what has troubled him or her.

Focus your mind on transmitting a thought-image to your pet. Perhaps you might try giving your pet a mental command, such as to fetch one of his or her favorite toys.

Visualize your pet walking toward the toy and bringing it to you.

Focus your mental energy on the visualization of this exercise being successfully completed. Spend at least two or three minutes seeking to transmit this mental command.

Remain silent and still as long as you and your pet can manage to do so. Seriously and as objectively as possible, evaluate the success of this experiment.

Did you receive what you believe to have been clear thought-images from your pet?

Did you feel that you gained any new insights into your pet's personality and mental-emotional makeup?

Did your pet respond to your mental command or suggestion?

Do you feel that you and your pet created a deeper bond by practicing this experiment?

Achieving Telepathic Transfer with Your Pet

Sit quietly by yourself for a few minutes before you attempt this exercise in telepathic transfer with your pet. You might visualize yourself as an ancient or traditional Native American finding a quiet, peaceful place in the forest in which to enter the silence.

Visualize the vastness of space.

Contemplate the measurelessness of time.

See yourself sending forth a beam of spiritual energy from your heart that grows and grows until it has encompassed and encircled all of nature, all of Earth. See your spiritual energy blending into a wonderful state of Oneness with the Great Mystery.

Now visualize your pet as the sovereign entity that it is.

See your pet before you in your mind's eye. Smell it. Hear it. Feel it. Be keenly aware of its spiritual essence.

In your mind, speak to your pet as if it were sitting or standing there beside you. Do not speak aloud. Speak mentally.

Breathe in three comfortably deep breaths. The act of breathing will help bring power to your mental broadcasting station.

Once again, mentally relay the message that you wish your pet to receive from you. Ask him or her to come to you.

Or perhaps ask your pet to bring you one of his or her favorite toys.

Continue to transmit your command to your pet for no more than five minutes.

This exercise will, in time and with repeated applications of mental energy, produce excellent results, but the exact amount of time required to achieve success with your pet depends on so many variables that it is best not to tire yourself on the very first attempt.

If you do not accomplish your goal of telepathic communication on the first try, repeat the experiment the next day—if at all possible, at the very same time.

Continue your experiments until you achieve the mind transfer necessary to complete a successful telepathic communication between you and your pet.

Send us your own animal miracles: Have you ever witnessed an unusual, heartwarming, or heroic deed by an animal or pet? We would like to hear about these personal events and possibly use them for an upcoming sequel.

Animal Miracles
Adams Media Corporation
260 Center Street
Holbrook, MA 02343

All submissions will become the property of Adams Media Corporation.